HELEN –

TO GOOD COOKING AND THE
THE KITCHEN. ENJOY THOSE DUFFY ROLLS!
MERRY CHRISTMAS

MY BEST,

12/17

The Party's
In the
Kitchen

For Steven A. Beyer

He was the light. Inspiring, caring and thoughtful. With his wit and heart he taught many of us the way. Man, I loved that guy.

WE ARE OUR ONLY ESCORTS DOWN THE ROAD

Somewhere I heard lyrics to a song that said that if you want to tell a story, you better sit down and start the damn writing. That's the scary part, telling stories verbally has its own rhythm by design. Writing them is about the same – like picking up a trombone for the first time and sticking it like you would with your well-used harmonica. Atonality and dissonance could lie dead ahead. But hell, this is about food and an illiterate can cook.

Cooking is about understanding proportion both visually and in flavor.

In her memoir, Out of Africa, Karen Blixen (Isak Dinesen) wrote about her many experiences living in British East Africa as a coffee plantation owner in the early 20th century. She notes often a fascinating individual, Kamante Gatura, a local tribesman who was, in her opinion and those of her many sophisticated guests from Western Europe, a culinary genius. His praises and reputation traveled back to the continent. The man never tasted the food he prepared. Ever. He preferred the tribal diet. Proportion was perfection, visually and aromatically and the results were brilliant.

Herein are the stories of my journey in the kitchen. It's about having fun and making good food with others who share a similar passion. They spend their days as teachers, artists, salespeople, etc. but not as food professionals. So, open some wine, give those measuring spoons to the little kiddies for toys, crank up the music and let's make some noise with those roasters, fry pans and kettles.

DOTY STREET AND BEYOND

In 1954, before memories evolved and I was still in diapers, our mother Agnes, my two older sisters Sally and Jane, and my older brother Bobbie (Rob) and I moved in with my grandparents, Michael and Mary (Mate) Cawley into their modest house on Doty Street.

It was a bit close for the seven of us but we never wanted for the necessities of life. And food was one at the top of the list. Michael and Mate were of Irish descent, and the kitchen was her domain until she passed away just shy of my tenth birthday. After her passing the menus and ingredients remained pretty much the same until the Duffey children began to scatter in 1966. Michael, Agnes and myself were the last to abandon ship on Doty Street in the spring of 1968. During those years the kitchen evolved into a self serve cooperative for the most part.

My grandpa was a story-teller. And I was a very attentive listener.

Michael Cawley left the Auld Sod as an early-middle-aged man, the youngest of eleven. He followed his brother Seamus, great uncle Jimmy (my namesake), and escaped the family farm in County Sligo, breaking his widowed father's heart. It was an involved route and itinerary, indeed. I was in a favorable position to hear elements of his odyssey, having so much time alone with him as a toddler.

Train rides that crisscrossed the homeland were, by necessity, very involved, due to the existing available routes. Many miles were walked, numerous short rides were taken on the back of animal-driven farmer's carts, and he even rode a mule for what was described as a "good trade out" with another countryman.

The trans-Atlantic voyage was crowded, and many arrived ill in America, only to be turned away in New York harbor where they were told too many Irish had arrived ahead of them at Ellis Island. They became freight forwarded to New Orleans. The Irish and New Orleans were no strangers to each other. Even with its St. Patrick's church towering over the bustling business district and familiar signs of Irish inhabitants, the city was very strange to Michael Cawley, who in his tweed cap, sport coat and knickers was equally a strange sight to two young men who asked him for his autograph, mistaking him for a world-class golfer. Even though his arrival preceded Bobby Jones, the preeminent golfer by twenty years as the game was growing in popularity in America.

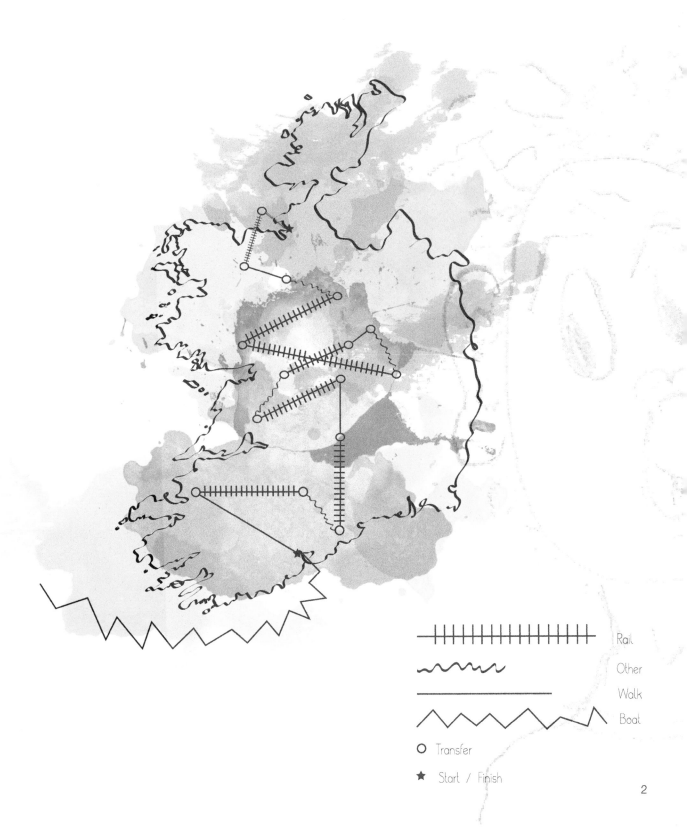

┼┼┼┼┼┼┼┼┼┼┼┼┼	Rail
∿∿∿∿∿∿∿∿	Other
——————	Walk
∧∧∧∧∧∧∧	Boat
○	Transfer
★	Start / Finish

Michael Cawley was exhausted and lonely; he needed to see his oldest brother. The trip north was taken by rail. After reuniting with him, Michael worked a variety of jobs as a back barman and a coal and ice deliveryman – and during those years, met his future mate, Mary McCabe. They married and had four children, the youngest of whom was my mother, Agnes.

As parents and throughout their lives, Michael and Mary never drove or wished to own a car. Gramps had a different plan. He passed the Civil Service exam and became a mail carrier, which he did the rest of his adult life until retirement. Security was paramount, and what was said among that genre of Irish was, "A true sign of success, more than owning a car – is how thick the slab of butter is that you can put on your slice of bread." The icebox/ fridge was deeply seeded in our hearts… and so was butter.

"Jimmy, it's a great life if you don't weaken," he often told me on those trips to and from kindergarten where he served as my escort and bodyguard. Our trip home from school took us by Millin's, the neighborhood grocer. That's where most of the sustenance came from, including the cuts of meat that were the centerpiece for Sunday dinner, as well as the list of items that were the full-time and occasional residents of Mary Cawley's domain, both cupboards and fridge:

Ice Box/Fridge Permanent Tenants:

Whole milk
Butter
Miracle Whip
Oscar Meyer bologna
Jelly
Pickles
Velveeta
Cabbage
Ice cream
French's mustard
Popsicles (seasonal)

Ice Box/Fridge/Occasional Tenants:

Sunday's leftovers
Frozen orange juice
Oscar Meyer wieners
Heinz Chili Sauce
Eggs and bacon
Oscar Meyer ham
Frozen french fries
Frozen fish sticks

IT'S JUST FOOD! WHO CARES?

The Cupboards Permanent Tenants:

Campbell's tomato soup
Large jar of creamy peanut butter
Premium saltines
Can of ground coffee
Assorted teas
Flour
Baking powder
Baking soda
Sugar
Salt and pepper
Chili powder

The Cupboards Occasional Tenants:

Campbell's vegetable beef soup
Campbells green pea soup
Canned stewed tomatoes (get to that issue later)
Canned sauerkraut
Canned sliced beets
Canned cream style corn
Canned tuna fish in oil
Canned salmon
Canned green peas
Canned kidney beans
Elbow macaroni
Flat egg noodles

The Bread Box:

There were more comings and goings here to differentiate,
but here are some inhabitants;

Bakery White Bread
Coffee Cake
Cinnamon Rolls (when just bought)
Sugar Wafers (they still exist)
Oreo Cookies
Graham Crackers

The Back Room of the Cellar:

Case of Fauerbach bottled beer
Currant jelly
Jarred tomatoes
Jarred pickled peaches
25 lb. sack of potatoes
And a peculiar assortment of other items in jars that
I couldn't discern from the accumulation of dust

These were the tools of the trade for Mate and
remained the same until we disbanded. Here is how
these treasures were put to use.

Time to Eat on Doty Street

Ring of Bologna with Green Beans

We used a 24 oz. Oscar Meyer Ring
Water to cover
2 15 oz. cans of green beans, juice included
4 mashed potatoes with butter, maybe some salt and pepper

1. Carefully place ring into enough water to cover and boil.
2. Best to have the potatoes ready to mash by now.
3. Beans are better if served hot but not burnt.

Goulash with Hamburger Meat and Velveeta

1 lb. or so of uncooked hamburger meat
1 lb. package of uncooked macaroni. (2 lb. if you want leftovers!)
4-5 slabs of sliced Velveeta cheese
1 15 oz. Campbell's tomato soup

1. Brown the heck out of the hamburger meat in a skillet, set aside.
2. Boil the begorra out of the macaroni, drain and set aside.
3. Open can of tomato soup and set aside.
4. Be careful while you slice the Velveeta not to cause deep lacerations.
5. Throw all of this stuff together in a large casserole dish and mix well.
6. Cook in the oven until the top starts to brown, but not too brown. Let cool for a few minutes.
7. Served with cooked, canned green peas.

Tuna Casserole

1 lb. bag of those flat egg noodles
1 big can of StarKist tuna in oil
1 can of Campbell's cream of mushroom soup
2-3 handfuls of potato chips, crushed

1. Boil the bejesus out of those noodles. Set aside.
2. Open can of tuna and drain the oil. Set aside.
3. Open can of soup and set aside.
4. This is very important: Mix the above 3 ingredients in the large casserole dish before you top with those potato chips.
5. Bake in oven until it looks right without burning the chips. Let cool for a while. Then serve.

Salmon Loaf

2 15 oz. canned salmon
15 Premium saltines, crushed with a rolling pin while wrapped in wax paper
1 cup real good cream
2 Tbsp of flour
1 egg
Salt and pepper to taste
15 oz. can of green peas

1. Open those cans of salmon. Spend at least 15 minutes fishing for the small bones that populate the salmon and discard. **DON'T MISS A BONE!** This could result in severe consequences at the table. Better to take care of now than require calls to Father Joyce or the medics. Set bones aside.
2. Mix together the boneless salmon, crushed saltines, egg, half the cream, salt and pepper in a bowl.
3. Form this mix into a loaf (like bread dough) and place in a bread-cooking pan. Put in oven and bake until done.
4. Meanwhile, in a saucepan, think about making a good gravy. Melt the butter and add the flour, continuously mixing. Never stop or you'll have a ball of crap. Add the rest of the cream, or more if needed, while mixing. When really nice and creamy, add the peas. Done!
5. Carefully remove the salmon loaf from the pan and let stand until it will cut into slices about like bread. Pour green pea sauce over the loaf. We like this with creamed style corn and bread with butter.

This was our highlight of the entire week for dining. It involved the most preparation both in time and ingredients. It was regaled with a formal setting of the dining room table, the liberation of all the best in flatware, china, glassware, tablecloths and linens from the auld country; nothing was spared. Their disappearance lasted for seven days until the following Sunday.

It started with the meat. Hams were roasted with cloves and glazed, pork roasts were seared, seasoned with salt and pepper and slices of butter and roasted, beef rump roasts were annihilated in the iconic aluminum cast pressure cooker with carrots and potatoes and so were massive beef sirloins with canned stewed tomatoes. We called this "Swiss Steak." This rotation was rarely interrupted except at Thanksgiving and Christmas when a 20-25 lb. Turkey was stuffed and carefully tended to for twelve hours.

Gravies were mates' specialties. Mashed potatoes were the typical accompaniment, except canned yams replaced them when ham was the centerpiece. A canned

vegetable was paired, and there was often a dinner roll that displaced the sliced bread. But there was always plenty of butter. This was also the day for desserts. Cakes were the norm – angel food with frosting and sprinkles, chocolate frosted with chocolate and the occasional surprise. Pies were made, but saved for the poultry dates aforementioned. But the true dignitary that came as a special guest to these occasions was Garrett's "Virginia Dare" American white wine, from the famous wine country of North Carolina.

Leftovers were paid special attention to. If not eaten for Monday's dinner, the meats were

ground in a cast aluminum meat grinder that I'd like to have my hands on now. It screwed onto a table like a vice and had a handle that turned, forcing the meat down into a wicked grinding wheel. Once ground up, Miracle Whip and pickle relish were added for the makings of sandwiches. Powerful stuff.

A COOKING JOURNEY

After comparing notes recently with my siblings, it was unanimously agreed that we disbanded the cooperative for all sorts of different reasons, and a bit of information was discovered. Our recollections of Doty Street Dining, right down to every detail were unanimous, just as described. We weren't nuts. None of us had ever seen or eaten a fresh green bean, a grilled steak, anything that included fresh garlic or a fresh garden salad before 1965. But memories of that pressure cooker were imbedded. No problem. Better exposed to these wonders over time when you are old enough to give a squat. So, how did this little group of siblings become crazed in the kitchen over time? Some of this family's creations are found herein. Others come from collaborating with the many friends who love playing around in the kitchen, always twisting and turning, and few of us who know what a "tablespoon full" actually looks like.

This is about cooking simple. One of my favorite cookbooks is Seriously Simple by Diane Rossen Worthington. It was a gift some years ago, and it is genius and the photography spectacular. She nailed it. If I can compare this work in any way, this book should be entitled "seriously, seriously, foolishly simple," lacking the craft of Noel Barnhurst's photography and salting in a bit of nonsense along the way.

All of my intrigue and passion for the goings on in the kitchen originated from hanging around with my sister Sally and her late husband, Steve. Steve was the instigator of all this craziness.

When a Friday afternoon rolled around in my early college days, the two of them would decide it was pizza night. That meant experimenting with different tomato species and spice combinations for the sauces. Doughs were made by hand with a variety of flours. Potatoes and toppings knew no bounds, and cheeses were sourced from out of town if Steve had returned from the road.

Steve and Sally gave me my first cookbook for Christmas, 1978, The Chinese Cookbook by Craig Claiborne and Virginia Lee. Off to the races. You could make better stuff than most of the best Chinese restaurants in the entire Midwest and enjoy the conviviality with friends while doing it in your own kitchen for a fraction of the cost... and a better variety of beer! Adaptations and changing things up were endorsed. So the word "recipe" should be used and practiced loosely herein. This is the result of experimentation and a lot playfulness in the kitchen. If you follow these recipes they might be just to your liking. But if it calls for some cumin and you love cumin, use more; conversely, if the thought of cumin puts

the whole notion on the skids, leave it out or use a small pinch. I have included dosages of the various ingredients to help along those that don't use a free hand and want some guidelines. It should make a good offering in the end, but you will, in time, give those measuring spoons to the little ones. Thanks to all of you who spent time in kitchens with me, teaching, sharing, laughing and making a big mess for me to clean up. Don't be afraid!

Fresh Sturgeon And Crappie Fish Stock Pg. 3069 & Hand Compressed Peanut Butter Infused with Whale Oils and Red Pepper Mayonnaise Aoli Pg 4,728

NEW ESSENTIALS

Fear of Cooking

6,000 NEW RECIPES

The Essentials

Some vintage oval aluminum roasters with lids. One big 8 qt. and a 6 qt. Wagnerware made of the old-timey Magnalite variety. These, or a facsimile, are a must. If you can't find these, there are a lot of similar ones sold at garage sales or online. A couple of all-aluminum skillets. 2 woks (and throw away the damn rings which are allegedly for safety), a big roasting pan for turkeys and ribs – about 12"x16"x3" should do. 2-3 Pyrex baking dishes, a Chinese cleaver, 3-4 good knives that you know how to sharpen, several sizes of wine glasses with a gel pen for ID, a perforated spoon from the same place you find woks – and we can assume you already have the other stuff like saucepans, whisks, etc.

A pantry of spices that hopefully you can buy in bulk from a place like cooperative farmers markets so that you don't have to take out a second on the Airstream because you're buying in miniscule quantities at the local supermarket's spice aisle at prices higher per oz. than top-shelf weed. You're going to be using these in small handfuls at times. And you can't find them when you make that trip to fishing camp in Wyoming or zip off for the holidays to South Dakota to join Uncle Nerf and Aunt Gehrky. Also, this list is minimal compared to what you might need if you get way off the trail – baking, making your own sausages, curing, canning, or following a strict religious diet.

PERMANENT CUPBOARD RESIDENTS:

Coarse sea salt

Coarse ground black pepper

Salt-free lemon pepper

Black sea salt

Garlic salt

Onion powder

Cinnamon

Cayenne

Ground sage

Cumin

Coriander

Nutmeg

Curry

Thyme

2-3 chili powders

Coarse Herbs de Provence

Thyme

Italian seasoning

Mexican oregano

Bay leaves

Sage

Fennel seeds

Rosemary

Red chile flakes

Unbleached all-purpose flour

Granulated sugar

Dark brown sugar

Natural brown sugar

Cornstarch

Baking powder

Yeast

Honey

Arborio rice

Long grain and wild rice

Medium grain white rice

Corn meal

Panko or seasoned bread crumbs

Low sodium chicken broth

Garbanzo beans

Beef consommé

Canned crushed tomatoes

Tomato paste

Your favorite ragu/tomato sauce

Pomi tomatoes

Thin spaghetti

Papparadelle

Penne

Olive oil

Canola oil

Peanut oil

Good balsamic vinegar

White vinegar

Red wine vinegar

Sesame oil

Lite soy sauce

Natural rice vinegar

Cooking spray for pans and grills.

Rubs. Will explain when in use. Never stop thinking about rubbing, especially the meats.

Flavored olive oils. Make them yourself and save a small fortune.

PERMANENT BASKET RESIDENTS:

Russet potatoes
Sweet potatoes
Lemons
Onions
Garlic bulbs
Big chunks of fresh ginger
Limes

PERMANENT FRIDGE RESIDENTS:

Dijon mustard
Ketchup
Capers
Basil pesto
Sundried tomato pesto
Thai peanut sauce
Lea & Perrins
Tabasco
Sriracha hot chili sauce
Chili garlic sauce
Pepto-Bismol
Red curry paste

Hoisin sauce
Butter
Guinness
Half and Half (fat free or the real stuff)
Salsa
Sour cream
Cream cheese
Parmesan cheese
Mozzarella cheese
A good Irish cheddar cheese
Pepperozzi peppers

*The Oval Office

The Recipes and their Tales,
Something Fishy

Mary's Sunday Salmon

For 2 people

This is the only way to cook fresh salmon. Baking is blasphemy. Grilling is a deathly poor idea. Nothing gets more screwed up than cooking good fish. Listen up. This will blow you away.

1 lb. wild salmon. Use the tail section, where the blood flows strongest for more protein and bones are infrequent.

1 Tbsp each of butter and olive oil (trying to help you out with portions here)

BBQ rub: about 2 Tbsp. You're going to lessen these portion recommendations as we go on (sea salt, paprika, onion powder, garlic salt, cayenne). A good substitute is Cajun seasoning

Some dark brown sugar...Get it!

Sriracha with garlic

Remember that aluminum-clad frying pan? Get it out. You're going **1** to use it a lot. And its lid.

Rub that salmon with the BBQ rub and dark brown sugar, don't be **2** afraid. Coat it generously and then put a light smear of Sriracha with garlic. You're set.

Into the frying pan with the butter and olive oil heated to medium **3** high, place the salmon (rubbed side down).

Cook at medium high heat for 4-5 minutes. It's critical to cook the **4** salmon until brown with the flesh side down, 4-5 minutes. Flip it to skin side down and cook at same heat for 3-4 minutes. While frying the salmon, cover most of the way with the lid.

The big move is to flip that salmon one more time so it's flesh side **5** down again. Remove the skin by grabbing it with a piece of paper towel. Flip again and cook 2 more minutes. Flip and love.

Fish Tacos

Making fish tacos has so many variations that all work. It's fun and should be done when you're surrounded by cooking friends. The choices of which fish to use, the cooking methods, condiments and spicing count into the hundreds. When we used to take our annual trips with friends and family to the Sea of Cortez south of Los Barilles, is when all of these possibilities arose. So did how to make ceviche and ahi. It was a toss-up what fish to use from the day's catch. Wahoo and dorado were perhaps best, but not always caught every day, making snapper (pargo) or sierra the usual choices. Some of you may know that dorado is the same as mahi-mahi, not hard to find.

3 lbs. fresh caught and cleaned, firm white-fleshed fish, skinned and cut into roughly one-inch squares.

Plastic zip bag closed and filled with:

2 cups unbleached flour

A generous amount of dark chili powder

Garlic salt

Cumin

Cayenne

The mixture's color should be a light orange or else you were uptight about the chili powder dosage.

Put those fish chunks into the bag, zipper it up and shake it, baby, until the cows come home, completely coating the fish. Toss into the fridge until I tell you it's time.

18 each, flour and corn tortillas. (If not making your own, buy uncooked and fresh from store.)

The stuff that can be put on these suckers to spice them up is endless. I'll give you 4 to try.

That reliable Thai Peanut Sauce.

Salsa Cruda: 1 Tbsp olive oil; 2-3 tomatoes, cored, seeds removed and finely chopped; a small bunch of fresh cilantro finely chopped; 1 small yellow onion finely chopped; 2 large garlic cloves finely chopped; 2 jalapenos minced; 1 Tbsp red wine vinegar or the juice of 2 key limes; 1 tsp of sugar and sea salt to taste. Sometimes we like to add chopped mango or fresh pineapple or a finely chopped Fuji apple. These last 3 are optional.

Yogurt Dressing: A 2-cup jar of plain yogurt, divided evenly. In one portion add the juice of 3 key limes and ¼ cup honey (or to taste); in the other, add a half cucumber that was peeled and finely chopped and, again, sweetened with honey.

Cole Slaw with Avocado Dressing: Blend 2 avocados, ¼ cup distilled vinegar, ¼ cup fresh cilantro leaves, juice of 1 lime, ½ cup plain yogurt, an 8 oz. can of pear or mango juice.

You're almost done. Easy out from here. Get all of your **1** condiments in order.

1 ½ cup canola oil into a wok. Heat on medium to high heat. Don't **2** let the oil get too hot to smoke you out of the kitchen. Toss in the dredged fish. Save that bag of seasoned flour in the freezer for next time.

Place the flour-coated fish into the oil and please don't overcook. **3** This takes 90 seconds. Use that perforated spoon to remove from the oil. Meanwhile, find an extra hand to fry the tortillas in an unsoiled pan. 45 seconds a side. Let it roll from here. It will.

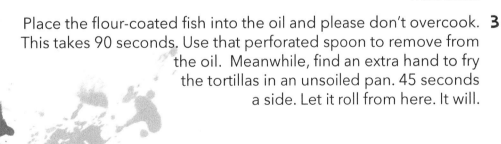

Ceviche

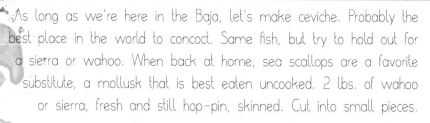

As long as we're here in the Baja, let's make ceviche. Probably the best place in the world to concoct. Same fish, but try to hold out for a sierra or wahoo. When back at home, sea scallops are a favorite substitute, a mollusk that is best eaten uncooked. 2 lbs. of wahoo or sierra, fresh and still hop-pin, skinned. Cut into small pieces.

Juice of 5-6 limes

Salsa Cruda (recipe above)

tsp of sugar

1 Into a container that will hold this stuff, add all ingredients, cover and refrigerate for 1 hour.

2 Ready to go. Serve with tortilla chips, saltines, out of your bare hands...makes no difference. Serve an hour before any main course with cold Pacifico beer.

Scallops with Sally's Bacon Jam

For 4 people

You're not going to find bacon jam at Costco or the Piggly Wiggly. Make this yourself and thank us forever. This can make an old sock a culinary masterpiece. Use this if you can.

Bacon Jam. Hmm-mm.

Sally follows the Sun Maid raisins recipe, which is available online with certain modifications, namely the addition of coffee and other secrets undivulged. (Other great recipes for bacon jam can be found if you search.)

For the scallops, simply sear 1 ½ lbs. sea scallops in 2-3 Tbsp olive oil.

Finish with 3 Tbsp of heated bacon jam.

We like to serve this with sautéed fresh green beans in olive oil and lemon zest.

Sea Bass with a Buzz Sauce

Get your hands on a fresh sea bass or Atlantic striper from the autumn waters of the North Atlantic and you are set. Markets sell this stuff seasonally as well. I realize the proponents who prefer baking will war against my darling skillets. Try it both ways, I swear by the skillet. The idea is to never overcook fish, seafood, chicken, beef or pork. And control is best exercised with the stovetop.

2 lbs. of sea bass, skin removed. Cut into ½ lb. pieces. If you have a phobia about sharpening or using sharp knives, find a nice butcher, tell him how nice he/she is, give him/her a dollar and ask if they'll skin it for you – they'll be glad to.

1 cup of balsamic vinegar reduced in a saucepan over medium heat to a "syrup." When it starts to bubble, reduce to about ⅓ cup. Set aside.

2 Tbsp butter

Juice of half lemon, 3-4 cloves of garlic, smashed with the cleaver, skin removed and very coarsely chopped.

2 Tbsp Lea & Perrins

2 Tbsp each of butter and olive oil

2-3 Tbsp of peach, pear chutney or currant jelly. Any one of these will make this work.

Into the balsamic syrup add the 2 Tbsp butter, lemon juice, garlic, Lea & Perrins and chutney/jelly, Whisk over medium heat until it starts to thicken. Taste this stuff and adjust to your own preferences. This is a wild sauce, a perfect match for wild fowl as well. Set on low simmer. **1**

Melt the butter/oil and pan-fry the bass/striper over medium high heat, 2-3 minutes a side. Check it to make sure it's cooked enough but never overcooked. **2**

Sauce over fish. **3**

Coquilles St Jacques

This one will spike that LDL. I can't understand why other renditions of this are extremely complicated. This is easy and promises to make folks squawk for more.

NOTE: Before you start, find/buy 8-12 large scallop shells. They sell them at specialty cookware stores. They last forever.

1 lb. 20-24 shrimp, peeled, deveined and set aside

1 lb. sea scallops, about the same size as the shrimp (not the little pea-sized bay scallops)

4 garlic cloves, smashed, skin removed and coarsely chopped

4 Tbsp butter

1-2 Tbsp flour

5-6 slices of good Swiss cheese, Tillamook's 3.5"X3.5" will do.

½ cup mid-shelf chardonnay

1 pint fat-free Half and Half

3-4 Tbsp Parmesan cheese, some good stuff, shaved

3 dashes sea salt

Breadcrumbs

Cayenne

Canola cooking spray

1 Make the roux. If you've never done this, ask a buddy to help you who's done this before. It always unnerves people when they have what looks like a yellow ball of glump. It's OK. That's what it's supposed to look like in the early stage.

The roux is made by melting the butter at medium heat and adding the flour while whisking this glump like a crazed weasel. Next, start adding the Half and Half, weasel… and the white wine until smooth. Turn down to medium low. The roux should have no lumps and not have a glump of flour anywhere in the pan. The hardest part of the entire preparation is now over. Have some of that chardonnay in one hand and start adding the Swiss slices one at a time, whisking constantly until it's all in and you've kept the consistency. Add ½ the shaved Parmesan and sea salt. Like it? Cover and set it aside.

2 Serious stuff here. Never, never overcook seafood, fish, beef, pork or others unless instructed. Those instances will be obvious and annotated. (A hint for the dull-minded: Pork Spare Ribs, Halloween Chicken, Pork Carnitas, All-Day-Long Beef Stew, and others you'll encounter here.)

You're now going to sauté the sea scallops and shrimp in the olive oil and butter. In that clad frying pan, heat the oil and butter to medium high heat. Before you turn the kitchen into a smoking inferno, fry the mixture of seafood for 1 minute. Toss in the garlic and fry another minute. Add the sea salt and remove from the heat.

3 Into those beautiful shells lathered up with the oil spray and resting precariously on a large baking sheet, add 2-3 Tbsp of the roux. Now, depending on the shell count and attitude of the cook, evenly distribute the seafood sauté. More seafood, more shells. Add the rest of the roux until your cup is full, but not runneth over. Add as you like the remaining Parmesan, breadcrumbs and cayenne to taste (and color). We're cooks, remember?

4 Bake at 425 degrees for 12-15 minutes, then broil for 2 minutes. Done.

5 Pair with your favorite veg and /or starch. Caesar Salad and wild rice comes to mind.

Red Clam Spaghetti

For 3-4 people who like Quickies

1 large can Geisha whole baby clams

1 big can of crushed tomatoes. Here, I suggest Muir Glenn fire roasted.

5-6 garlic cloves, chop a little bit more than previously suggested.

¼ cup red wine. Suggest a pinot or "sweeter" red blend than we drink at the table.

1 big pinch of sugar

Sea salt to taste

½ lb. cooked thin spaghetti, al dente

1 In the same skillet, pour the juice from the can of clams and add the garlic.

2 Sauté until reduced by about half. Never, never overcook or brown the garlic. Add the tomatoes, red wine, and continue to cook at medium high until things start to thicken, stirring attentively. Add the clams, sugar and salt. This will thicken quickly over medium heat for 4-5 minutes.

3 Serve with spaghetti.

Chinese Shrimp with Peanuts

For 4 people

2 lbs. shrimp – big suckers, fresh as you can find, peeled, deveined and patted dry

2 Tbsp each of cornstarch, Shao Hsing wine

6 Tbsp peanut oil

4 scallions, green to white, sliced thin

3 Tbsp chopped fresh ginger

6 garlic cloves, peeled, smashed with the flat side of the cleaver and coarsely chopped

2 Tbsp each of lite soy, ketchup, Shao Hsing wine (dry sherry if necessary), Sriracha with garlic, 2 tsp sugar, 1 Tbsp sesame oil – all mixed together

½ cup or more of raw, unsalted peanuts

1 Mix cornstarch and wine together thoroughly and add shrimp. Refrigerate for half an hour.

2 Heat peanut oil over medium heat and cook peanuts for 2 minutes, never letting them brown as they keep cooking after pouring the peanuts into a colander over a bowl to capture all the oil.

3 Peanut oil goes into a wok. Get all the other ingredients lined up, ready to go.

4 Heat the oil for 1 minute over high heat and add the shrimp mixture. Stir fry for about 2 minutes.

5 When things are getting hectic and noisy, add the garlic and ginger, continue stir frying for another minute.

6 Add the soy mixture and blanched peanuts. Keep stirring for another 1-2 minutes. Take off the flame and add the scallions. Done.

7 By now, I hope you realize that your rice preference was cooked and our favorite pairing from buds and spuds (stir fried snow peas with sesame oil) were, as well.

Pan Fried Sole with Chive Lemon Sauce

There are very few things herein that don't allow for a certain margin of error, forgiveness for having a few swigs of wine with your guests, checking out a hockey score, wandering out to the garden...except this gem. Complete attentiveness required. If it's not your style to comply, make Beef Stew or Halloween Chicken. Enough time tending those to read Ulysses. Pick a bud and spud that can rest while you make this one.

2 lbs. fresh sole, about 8 fillets

Breadcrumbs of your choice, Panko, Progresso, whatever; I prefer corn meal.

2 eggs stirred up in a wide flat bowl big enough for those sole fillets to take their last swim.

4 Tbsp of butter for sautéing

1 ½ Tbsp butter for roux

1 tsp flour

½ cup or so of Half and Half (fat full or free)

2 tsp each of lemon juice and dry white wine, the one you have in your other hand will do

2 Tbsp fresh finely chopped chives

1 Remember that roux? Melt butter in small saucepan over medium heat. When melted – but never burnt – add the flour, stirring wildly (hopefully you can put the wine down for a moment). Just as this turns into the pile of goo, start adding the Half and Half. Stir with the same arm you use to... a.... throw a frisbee until smooth and creamy thick. Add the wine, lemon juice and chives. One small dash of coarse sea salt is optional. Remove from heat and keep warm.

2 A deft hand and 2 skillets are now required. After washing the sole fillets in the egg, thoroughly dredge in the breadcrumbs/cornmeal. Very important that the fillets are completely coated. This is when it helps to have a good cohort. Melt 2 Tbsp of butter in each pan over medium/medium high heat. (It's good to learn about your stove top – the target temp is 350-375.) Sauté the sole for about 1 minute per side until light golden brown. Remove from heat, plate and spoon with the sauce.

Pan Seared Halibut Fillets

Halibut, flounder, striped sea bass and a lot of other fish and seafood we cook are only available fresh on a seasonal basis. Be persistent in trying to find the best source for these year round. If you have to substitute because of lack of availability, be wise with your choice. Some of the non-domestic farm-raised varieties have dubious nutritional value and employ very sketchy sanitation procedures. Like all of the fresh fish recipes, preparation of your buds and spuds or other accompaniments must be finished and ready to serve once you are ready to pan fry the fish.

4 8-oz. pieces of fresh halibut fillets

6 Tbsp olive oil

4 cloves minced garlic

Sea salt, black pepper, and juice of one lemon

3 Tbsp butter

2 Tbsp Worcestershire (Lea & Perrins. Just a plug for these guys. For 180 years they have put out a product with all-natural ingredients that is terrific.) I'm not a fan of prepared dressings and sauces that read like a chemical engineer's PhD thesis.

2 cloves of crushed and coarsely chopped garlic

2 Tbsp currant jelly or orange marmalade

Cayenne pepper

3 scallions, finely chopped, green included

1 Pat dry the halibut fillets and place in a shallow glass dish large enough to hold them. Mix the olive oil, minced garlic, and salt and pepper in a bowl and pour over the fillets and refrigerate for 1 hour.

2 In a small skillet melt the butter and add the Lea & Perrins, garlic, a pinch of cayenne and the jelly or marmalade of your choice on low heat. Cook for 5-7 minutes until sauce thickens and add the scallions. Keep at very low heat until fish is prepared

3 In a large skillet to fit the fillets, melt 2 Tbsp of additional butter and some of that olive oil from the marinade. Sear fry the fish fillets on medium high heat for about 2-3 minutes per side. Let things get fried up and brown on the outside but not overdone. Plate the fish and serve with the warmed sauce.

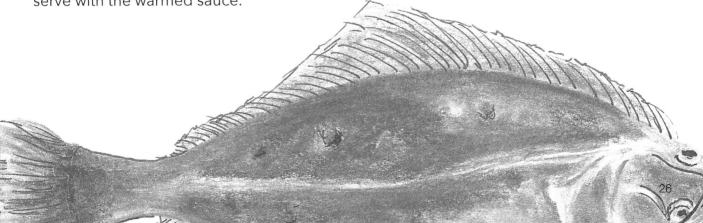

Cashew Crusted Flounder

A word about eating both flounder and sole, two of our very favorites. I am not an ethologist, but both are facing serious consequences of overfishing and pollution of estuarial waters. Same can be said for our favorite seafoods. Extol the flavor of wild caught and decry the lack of flavor in farm raised and their practices, but we have to take measure and moderate. People garden for their own enjoyment and consumption and keep their own chickens for egg production in the city centers, but it's a problem to harvest shrimp, sea bass and flounder out of the Highline Canal or East River. Make these memorable occasions. Or go find a local catch that you've overlooked.

4 6-8 oz. flounder fillets

1 cup unsalted cashew pieces

1 cup breadcrumbs

2 Tbsp finely chopped chives

2 Tbsp melted butter

Sea salt

Olive oil and additional butter for pan frying

1 Chop the cashew pieces finely and add to the breadcrumbs. Add the melted butter and chives to the cashew mixture and blend well with a fork. Place the mixture on wax or parchment paper and coat both sides of the fish fillets by firmly pressing to the flesh.

2 Melt additional butter in a fry pan large enough to hold all the fillets and add the olive oil over moderate to high heat. Carefully place the fillets in the fry pan when the oils are hot but not smoking. Fry for 2-3 minutes per side to a nice golden brown and serve at once. You have it right if there is a good crust formed on each side and the flounder is moist and tender.

THE ARC, OCD, WITH OTHER MEN IN THE KITCHEN

The vast, experimental cooking events occurred with my wife Mary. Thank the lord she is a patient, beautiful and gracious women. I won the Wife Lottery. However, many of my inspired experiences in the kitchen went down with other male cooks. They are the people who moved the charts. Steve, Will, Jimmy, Dazey, Paddy and Eddy were the real influences. Now, there were issues. Taping off windows and adjacent rooms, covering the floors, and wearing complete body coverings were, at times, not enough. These pals were rapacious, swinging, chopping, messy and inspirational. My natural instincts as ARC (Anal Retentive Cook) meant that I followed closely behind, sweeping,

wiping, washing, and engaging in unnatural behavior to keep the ordinance of the kitchen from looking, minimally, like a complete breakdown of order! I am also OCD, by the way. These lovely men had to endure hanging with the Anal Retentive Cook and an OCD-affected guy! Bad disorder.

Now, knowing my reality, imagine the stuff hitting the walls - well beyond fans, exhaust or otherwise. These were a collective of ex-college football, hockey and rugby players, marginal criminals (jokingly of course), and the smartest group of men in the kitchen I know. They "attacked" cooking, cleavers flashing,

knives flying, and (my issue) floor accumulating piles of unwanted vegetable and meat parcels.

It works, and continues to work, we will note their amazing talents and contributions where applicable going forward.

HOW TO BE A REAL DIP

We have found these two to be most versatile, earning full time residency in our fridge. They're Asian in origin, but can be used in countless ways – for Chinese dumplings, spring rolls, as marinades and sauce for meats, for seafood and more. They are a requirement. When our son was about 12 years in the making, he discovered our Thai Peanut Sauce was to be integrated wherever possible. It was used in as ubiquitous a fashion as most kids use ketchup and mustard. We used to smuggle it into Mexico along with a few other contraband in our dive bags and labeled in boxes as "sink tip reel" or "defogger." We'll give you the mandatory ingredients, followed by a list that can be added singularly or as you wish. These are standard small batches, about 12 oz.

DIP #2 Thai Peanut Sauce

½ cup peanut butter
½ cup sweetened coconut milk
3 Tbsp fresh lime juice
3 Tbsp lite soy sauce
3 clove garlic, peeled and skinned
1 ½ tsp coriander
1 ½ tsp cumin
1 tsp Sriracha sauce

1 Blend all ingredients in a blender for 2 minutes until very smooth.

2 Every time we make this, we'll taste it and attenuate to suit our mood.

3 Here are some items to consider as additions or substitutes: Use brown sugar and Half & Half in place of the coconut milk. 2 crushed dried red chilies, seeds removed, in place of Sriracha. More garlic! Here's a sleeper: harissa paste and if you get some of this that's well made, use sparingly. We use Savory Accents Brand from Verona, WI.

DIP #1 Green River Sauce

½ cup light soy sauce
½ cup rice vinegar, all natural, sodium and sugar free
3 Tbsp minced garlic
3 Tbsp minced ginger
1 ½ Tbsp sugar
1 tsp chili oil
1 tsp pure sesame oil
2-3 finely chopped scallions

1 Nothing complicated here. Mix it well so sugar is dissolved.

2 Refrigerates well for 2 weeks.

Whacky Spring Rolls

There were days when the crew would set up in the kitchen and make our own pork dumplings and spring rolls. We bought our skins from the Asian markets out of the fridge case, locally made, but everything conjured up from there was purely spontaneous. Every combination was encouraged, and the slagging between us was ruthless. Beer-drinking was fostered. We'll spell out a list of items that were enclosed in these wonders after several sessions. Strongly suggest make a day out of this yourselves. You'll find and... lose your way.

Anybody can reference how to roll your own rolls and pinch up dumplings. Frying and boiling techniques, same. Look at this list and build your own. Hope you add some of your own ingredients in time.

Fresh bean sprouts

Chopped cabbage

8 dried black mushrooms, soaked in hot water, drained and chopped

½ cup BBQ Chinese pork, chopped

3 scallions, green part included, chopped

3 Tbsp chopped fresh cilantro

¼ lb raw salmon, finely chopped

½ cup finely diced fresh shrimp

¼ cup finely minced ham

¼ cup cooked Chinese duck finely chopped

5 celery cabbage leaves, finely chopped

½ cup finely chopped pumpkin (dynamite!)

⅓ cup finely chopped peanuts, cashews

Have any combo of these items set to roll and you are ready. These are guaranteed to be special events, like 'pizza nights'.

NO IRISH POPE?
PART 1: GOING HOME

S HEILA FITZGERALD WAS GOING home to her older brother's wedding. It had been over a year and a half since she had been to the modest family home in rural County Limerick. She was 20 years old, studying and working in San Francisco, intent on getting her Cosmetology certification in the U.S. John Lennon was now imagining as a resident of NYC. The aftermath of the Attica rebellion still haunted many.

Boarding this Aer Lingus red-eye from Kennedy to Shannon was a breeze for me. I held a round trip student standby ticket and the flight was half full. I was flush, $350 in cash from working the apple fields outside Princeton, NJ and grubbing at the Tiger House at the university. Finding a seat next to Sheila was a combination of luck and avarice. She was attractive and open to the options of whom to allow to be seated next to her. She was a vibrant red-haired, fair-skinned, blue-eyed lass full of piss about the trip back home.

I was four months prior to my nineteenth birthday. Amid seating and a quick introduction, I was unaware that the ability to make good judgments is reserved for those who have a fully developed frontal lobe. This was discovered sometime later in life. And being a male, it was a further handicap. Things like remembering names and making proper decisions were nebulous.

It seemed like a good idea to both of us to celebrate this flight with a few Guinnesses, complimentary of course. Sheila was amused by my inky plans to visit Ireland for the first time. I was motivated by writings of expatriate writers like J. P. Dunleavy and natives Yeats and Joyce (the last of whom I lied about completely as an author I admired). Reading Ulysses was a nightmare in Prepsterhood. Dylan Thomas was more my style but not mentioned. A Welshman. There was also the foggy, bullshit and insincere issues about going to find my family roots in Sligo and beyond. In short, I was just an unruly, youthful American, a vagabond looking to have a little adventure.

Sheila, I discovered during the seven-hour flight, was unlike the girls I had known. She had a direction, velocity and intent. She also asked if I wanted to go home with her as a guest for the upcoming nuptials. I believe it was something written by Dunleavy, paraphrased here, but something the male 18-year-old mind vaguely understood or heard, "When the going is too good to be true, reverse course and beat it, when the going is too hard to be true, forge on." I wasn't listening.

We landed at Shannon. It was early dawn and the view offered a very dimly-lit bay as we landed. Sheila and I were the most animated of all aboard. She told me her Mum was going to meet her at the airport and drive her home. They had a lot to catch up on but she invited me to come along with her for the ride home. Of course, I thought that was a great idea. Of course.

It was a small car. Mrs. Fitz met Sheila, bags were gathered and without much ado, I was the back seat passenger en-route to a big time family to-do...The Wedding. Amidst the efficient gathering of information that only women can do in such a short time, I had been introduced by Sheila as "James, my friend from America." Details were omitted. I could have been anybody in her life. She looked back at me on that ride as we circumnavigated Limerick City and winked and smiled with a shrug. Just one of these signs was tossing me, but three and four were testing my awareness. Maybe it was jet lag. I had heard about it, but have to this day no understanding of what it is. The frontal lobe was inoperative.

Mrs. Fitz had a personality I had not encountered. With the girls I had known to this point, when I met their moms, it was soon an uncomfortable scene. I was interviewed with suspicion and felt soon to be incarcerated. I made a note. My buddies' moms loved me and engaged me in lengthy and interesting conversations. What had I done? Must have been an odor. Mrs. Fitz, though, was thrilled I was coming to join them for the upcoming celebration. Ah, Ireland.

I've been told some pretty heady stuff over the years about the frontal lobe of the brain and its development. Things about making judgments requires this part of your noodle to be completely developed, and males take about four years longer than gals to get wired up properly; age twenty-four is a guess, if ever. But what is judgment? In Webster's Big Dict. they state, "the power to compare ideas and ascertain the relations of terms and propositions; understanding; good sense." Simple crap like asking someone to repeat something that was said that you didn't hear or understand, like a name or engaging in witless small talk. It seemed like we traveled about another thirty minutes southward before the front seat passengers started to quicken their discussions about what was going on in the small farms we were passing. Updates abounded and the currency of gossip was trading heavily as the session neared its final bell. We were close to Sheila's homecoming. I was given a quick update on who I was shortly to meet: an unmarried older sister, Mr. Fitz, two brothers – one older (soon to be wed) and one younger (the latter I was told was very close to my age). I was always overly interested in geography and how to set my coordinates. Where I was exactly in relation to this and that. Upon arrival at the Fitzgerald property I had no idea where the hell I was.

We parked in the front of a larger house than most I had seen along the past many miles. It was a large two-story white building with gas pumps in front. This was a 1971 Irish 7-Eleven. Buy some gas, buy some essentials in the little store front, and be on your merry way. Sheila and Mrs. Fitz were excited, as many reunions were imminent. First was father greeting daughter. I exited the car and stood silently until my introduction. Mr. Fitz was cordial but without any doubt, assumed I was Sheila's beau, arriving to join in the big wedding celebration. I didn't agree or deny any of what was said. Judgment again.

The siblings emerged and were now surrounding Sheila with hugs and kisses. Being sleepless for over twenty-four hours wasn't helping me follow the rapid dialogues being bantered about the front driveway. But the dialect, which was mutually intelligible among the Fitz clan, was not aimed at me anyway. My introductions to the rest of the group were quick – and peculiar. Things weren't clear. Knowing how to take measurements and never making assumptions was not a developed part of my intelligence. Not using these skills can be a disaster. Curiosities concerning my background and presence were non-existent. And, for my part, I only remembered Sheila's sister's name.

Mrs. Fitz ran this show. She asked the younger brother to take me inside and show me where I would be accommodated. This was in the rear of the building at ground level, a room that had a door to the grounds behind the house. It had three beds and my quiet host pointed to the one in the corner, "That's for ya."

"Tanks," I replied.

My host departed and I was alone for the first time since waiting for my name to be called as a standby passenger in New York. I looked at my U.S. Navy official canvas duffel bag, compliments of my brother-in-law Steve. Without its wrinkled contents the damn thing weighed fifteen pounds and was sturdy as hell. I thought about where this haute piece of luggage had been in the early 1950's when Steve marauded around the world as a submarine inhabitant for the better part of two years. It had been many places around the globe but never in this part of Ireland, where the road signs were nearly all written in Gaelic. Five directional signs at a random intersection stacked on top of each other, on a single pole, so many km to here, so many km to there, looked like a Christmas tree. 82 km to Corcaigh thataway, 75km to Ciarraigh thisaway. Yup, no clue where I was. The duffel has new digs.

I spent but a short moment alone before Mrs. Fitz asked if I'd like a bite to eat. That part of my fragile brain, telling me calories might be a good idea, had not yet made the connection until the invitation to join some of the family came up. The "dining room" turned out to be a very spacious area outside of my digs on the main floor with a table that easily could seat ten to twelve adults. The servings were fresh Sultana bread with lashings of butter, some hard cheeses, jams, and various cuts of meat. Who needed cheese when the butter that was so sweet and complex. During this repast, the first interrogations about my whereabouts began. "Where are you from, exactly? Is that near Chicago or San Francisco? Do you have family? Are any here in Ireland?" All lob balls. Nothing that would pin me down or point me in the direction of Sheila, yet. It was a business lunch, not of the power variety.

Sheila asked if she and I could be pardoned so she could show me around the property and then give me some time for a rest. We were excused and she tossed her head in the direction of a side door I had not yet noticed. It exited right from the dining room. Once outside, she asked how I was doing with "all of this." Again, she smiled and winked at me as she shook her head. I didn't know if she was attracted to me or not, but she sure was having fun with this charade. And for that, I found her a very interesting lass. She said her Mum thought I was a charming fellow and had told her to let me know that I was very welcome to stay for the wedding and enjoy a true Irish celebration, without any reservation. I said I was flattered by the invitation and would love to stay.

Sheila pointed out a few small outbuildings, a little slough with a small stream that entered and exited parallel to the road in front of their property. I noticed a small plot of stones that was located about halfway from the rear entrance where my new digs were and the slough. I asked her what that collection was. She said they represented a variety of things about the

family and some of them she said were new since she left for schooling in America.

She showed me to the door in the rear entrance where my quarters were now established with her younger brother. I thought it was the perfect time for a little rest. She squeezed my hand and laughed before she turned and walked away. It was our first physical contact. I found my bed and used my duffel as a pillow and dozed without a worry in the world.

When I woke I was surprised to see there was remaining daylight so I figured it was a good time to view the grounds behind the Fitzgerald's building to maybe discover some vital historical information or come across a point of interest. I was curious about the possible presence of eels that Grandpa Michael told me were common as a boy in the streams surrounding his family farm in Sligo. My wit regarding biology, especially for aquatic inhabitants of varietal waterways was actually better than most who lacked advanced higher education. I had lived most of my youth in a watery, mystical world beneath the surfaces. I saw there were no pots or buckets described by Gramps to trap eels. The whole waterway appeared lifeless. Here was something interesting: a cement stone about four feet square with the inscription "MOSSIE." Must have been a gravesite of sorts, a commemorative for a dog, or a pig or some other lost and coveted livestock that someone carefully inscribed on the lost one's behalf.

When I wandered back to the house, I met Mr. Fitz as he rounded to the back and asked if I had a nice walk and was invited to join the men of the house for a jar. We had some time to visit while Mrs. Fitz and the other women scurried to boil up some spuds and buds, as well as finish a pork roast from the oven. Ah, man talk. Discovery and interrogation at last. This was a comforting prospect with my first glass on the Ancient Island sharing our life histories. All vitals were shared: how long they had lived on this property; yes, I just met Sheila

on the plane and we were not an item; details about the bride and groom to be; I was still a welcomed member of the family; are you interested in a little of the Holy Water before dinner; of course… and so it went.

Blessed with new strength, I wanted to ask a few questions to show my interest in the Fitz family. I talked about my wanderings on the grounds behind the house, commented on the benign subject of eels and such and asked, "Is MOSSIE the name of a dead dog or pig or other – did I cross a commemorative?"

A silence ensued. Mr. Fitz asked me to repeat what I was saying. I repeated my question with a little more clear and audible annunciation. "Mossie," Sheila's brother and my bunkie said, "You bastard." More silence. Judgment.

AN OINK CANNOT BE DESCRIBED,
A CHICKEN CLUCKS

It was the late Jim Harrison, the brilliant American author who wrote something, somewhere. I've read so much of this man's work, it has blended together, and food was often a subject he wrote about. I think it was in Esquire, but it struck my funny bone. "Where are the thighs?" he wrote. Funny stuff. Americans were late to discover the boneless, skinless chicken thigh as a moral issue. He mused they were too close to the groin area, puritanical perhaps. Made me laugh and reflect. Chicken thighs are the best part of the chicken, and we use them almost exclusively, unless prescribed otherwise. But they were inexplicably unavailable in major markets in the 80's and early 90's and certainly before. Now available, I almost always butterfly these to the same thickness with my Chinese cleaver and cross-cut them 1/8" to further tenderize for all their uses. When we use chicken breast cuts for items like chicken Marsala, Parmesan or piccata, unless you are patient and deft with a knife, I suggest Perdue's thin cutlets. They're cut and seal-packaged masterfully. If not available, I would find a facsimile. And last, ground chicken is being substituted for beef more and more in my kitchen - for great burgers, balls and lettuce wraps, to name a few. Ground turkey and ground chicken thighs are interchangeable for those.

Pig is a pig of a different color. We've cooked every body part, and beyond a few surprises, we have rarely been disappointed. Just a quick take on cooking pork. Cook it quick and serve medium to medium rare with lean cuts like tenderloin and lean chops, but let the spices, sauces or marinades do the rest of the talking. When cooking the fattier and more robust cuts, cook all day long if need be to absorb the savories, smoke and seasonings until it falls apart effortlessly.

When sourcing meats such as pork sausages, sirloins and fine meats in general, make an effort to find the best. On one of my first trips back to Philadelphia decades ago to visit Mary's family, I was introduced to the 9th St. Italian Market, an American treasure. That's when I discovered Fiorella's, makers of the finest sweet or hot fennel sausages. I found them on one of my meanderings off the main thoroughfare. I was a sucker for a neon pig hanging over the sidewalk.

Mary's Bleu Balls

For 4 people

These were served to us in a restaurant about a year or so ago, and Mary has perfected them with just a few twists from how they were described. Think Cordon Bleu Meatballs.

The Balls:

1 ½ lbs. Lean ground chicken

¼ cup finely grated Parmesan or Locatella

¼ cup Italian style bread crumbs. Save time, money and brain damage, just use Progresso

¼ cup finely chopped fresh parsley

3 cloves of garlic, chopped finer than usual

1 egg

Sea Salt to your liking, start with a ½ Tsp

4 slices Prosciutto cut into 12 portions

4 slices Gruyere Cheese portioned equal to the Prosciutto

The Sauce:

1 Tbsp butter

1 Tbsp flour

¼ cup white wine (remember the roux?)

1 cup low-sodium chicken broth

½ cup cream, if necessary use fat-free Half & Half

1 Tbsp Dijon mustard

Juice of one large lemon

Sea salt to taste, start with ¼ tsp

Course black pepper to taste

1 Tbsp fresh finely chopped parsley or tarragon...or both

In a bowl, combine the ground chicken, Parmesan cheese, egg, parsley, **1** bread crumbs, garlic and salt. Mix well.

Make the sauce after you have formed the meatballs (see below). You want **2** the meatballs to jump straight from the oven into the pool of sauce. Heat together for 5 minutes before serving. Test the meatballs to make sure they are just past the pink stage, but not overcooked, before taking them for their swim.

Make 12 meatballs of equal size and stuff with an equal amount of the **3** prosciutto and gruyere, easy enough to punch a hole in each meatball with your index finger and close them back up. The important step is to bake these at around 425 degrees for only about 15-20 minutes on a baking sheet sprayed with oil. They want to be slightly browned but not overcooked.

The sauce is simple if you remember the roux approach. In a skillet, melt **4** the butter at medium heat, add the flour and whisk, whisk and whisk until the glump starts to form. And then add the wine, continue to whisk and add the broth and cream and continue until things are thickening and even in consistency. Then turn up the heat slightly and whisk in the mustard, lemon juice, sea salt, and pepper. Cover and set aside. When the meatballs are done, add to the sauce and simmer on low heat for 2-3 minutes and serve. Great with thin spaghetti seasoned with lemon and olive oil.

Chicken Burgers

A few words about chicken burgers. In our opinion, like so many other proteins, they should only be pan fried and never overcooked. Medium high heat, 2-3 minutes a side, partially covered with a fitted lid. We'll give you the basic cooking technique and give a list beyond the Basic Recipe (to follow) that you can ponder as options/additions. Naked if you wish, or on hearty wheat buns, as we prefer.

Good fresh ground chicken is like the flour and water paste we made in grade school. Sticky is good. We always pre-mix these ingredients in a suitable bowl before making them into burgers or wraps. I suggest using wet hands when forming the meat into patties. 3 patties per pound is the best size we've found. The Basic Recipe is: season your burgers with salt-free lemon pepper, a dash of garlic powder and 2 turns of coarse sea salt. Season the first side and add to the skillet at medium high heat, seasoned side down. Season the second side before you give them the flip. You're going to have to learn how long to cook these suckers by testing. Just past pink and still moist means done. If you start to choke to death on the first bite you've screwed up. We've followed the Basic Recipe with some great variations.

Toppings for the Basic Recipe:

Smoked havarti, mayo and tomato

Fried mushrooms and gruyere

Sharp cheddar and Stubb's Honey Pecan BBQ Sauce...give that man some serious props.

Sour cream, horseradish, lemon and curry...mixed to taste.

The following lists are things to mix with the ground chicken before cooking the Basic (based on 1 lb makes 3). Adjust volumes according to your names in the pot.

An Asian Touch:

4 Tbsp finely chopped scallions

1 Tbsp sesame oil

1 Tbsp lite soy

1 Tbsp coarse brown sugar

1 tsp each of chopped garlic and fresh ginger

Best when topped with Thai Peanut Sauce

Latino:

1 small finely diced jalapeño

¼ cup finely chopped fresh cilantro

Garlic salt to taste

1 tsp hot New Mexico chili powder

Like Salsa Cruda with this one

East Indian:

It takes courage.

1 tsp each of curry powder, cumin, garam masala

1 Tbsp coarse brown sugar

1 tsp each of fresh chopped garlic and ginger

Scant amount of Harrisa paste

Top these mamas with cream cheese, warmed and softened to room temperature.

Italian:

½ cup finely chopped fresh basil

4-6 cloves coarsely chopped garlic

½ cup shaved Parmesan

Sliced smoked provolone

Marinated summertime tomatoes from "Buds and Spuds (Pg. 81)"

Sarah's Chicken Wraps

2 lbs. ground chicken

1 bunch finely chopped scallions, green included

4 Tbsp finely chopped fresh ginger

3 Tbsp dark brown sugar

2-3 Tbsp sesame oil

10-12 pieces of red leaf or romaine lettuce, cleaned and patted dry

Hoisin sauce

Thai peanut sauce

1 Mix all ingredients in a bowl except the lettuce and sauces.

2 Fry the ground chicken mixture in a little peanut oil until cooked to suit.

3 Make up like a lettuce taco and use the sauce of preference.

4 NOTE: We don't use soy or salt in the mix. The sauces will cover your salt cravings.

CHICKEN THIGHS A FEW WAYS

These four are favorites that seem to have worked for a wide audience. Remember the oval aluminum stove-top roasters? Time to drag them out. We use them for these and prepare the boneless, skinless thighs in the described way by butterfly-cutting and scoring. The approach is redundant, but the outcomes are far from it. The chicken should always be easily shredded to be done. For these, as well as nearly everything herein, I'll give measurements, but I've never followed them one day to the next. Never have. For some, this will be perfecto, but for those like us, it's based on a sense of proportion, and favored ingredients get the extra hand. Become a cook for your own flavor preferences.

Chicken Enchiladas

2 lbs. boneless, skinless chicken thighs

3 Tbsp olive oil

6-7 garlic cloves coarsely chopped

1 cup of Salsa Cruda or your favorite store-bought variety of salsa, both work

1 cup low-sodium chicken broth

2 Tbsp dark chili powder

2 Tbsp light chili powder

3 Tbsp coarse dried Mexican oregano

2 Tbsp cinnamon

3 Tbsp coarse brown sugar

1 Tbsp ancho chile paste

4 oz pineapple juice

2 Tbsp cream cheese

½ cup coarsely chopped fresh cilantro

1 cup shredded Mexican cheese blend

More olive oil

12 fresh corn tortillas, preferably the kind you buy fresca, uncooked

1. Over medium high heat, cook the thighs in the olive oil until slightly browned. As they cook at this stage, break them into smaller pieces, no big deal.

2. Add the garlic and cook until transparent, never browned.

3. Keep that pot stirred and add the salsa and chicken broth. Continue to cook at medium high for 5-7 minutes.

4. Add the chili powders, oregano, cinnamon, brown sugar, ancho chile paste, and pineapple juice stirring continuously for 5 minutes.

5. Lower the heat and simmer at 200 degrees for 2 hours. Check that things aren't being overcooked and the chicken is coming apart easily with a fork. If needed, add more broth, but you want this to thicken. Drink a good cervesa and chill.

6. Regardless of where you sourced those corn tortillas, now is a good time to fry them in olive oil until soft, not browned, and layer on a plate.

7. The last steps for the finish of the chicken mixture is to add the cream cheese and cilantro and cook another 10 minutes. Mix well to disperse the cream cheese.

8. Spoon about 5 Tbsp of the liquid from the chicken mixture into a large 11" X 14" Pyrex dish.

9. Time to roll 'em up. Divide the cooked chicken mixture and wrap in the tortillas.

10. Cover with the cheese mixture once you've rolled them all up. Hopefully, there is come of the chick mix to spoon over the top.

11. Add the cheese, cover with foil and cook for 20-30 minutes at 350. When things are bubbling and acting up and the cheese has melted to your liking, remove and serve.

12. Like this with some Mexican rice recipe found in Buds and Spuds or refritos prepared with cooked crumbled bacon, garlic, olive oil, Sriracha and cinnamon.

Curry Chicken

When I was in my early twenties, I met a couple from Kerala, India. He was finishing a fellowship in medicine and we batted around tennis balls and played one-on-one hoops on certain weekends. But the real purpose for our get-together was to eat his wife's cooking and drink good beer. Her cooking always blew me away. Forget the merchandised "curry powders" that I recommend using; hers were an intricate blend of the hottest damn chiles and a multiplicity of fresh ground spices that varied per dish but, in general, included turmeric, nutmeg, coriander, cumin, ginger, garlic and others. She explained to me that her region of Kerala had its own slant on ingredients, and the southwestern edge of India tended to be a little spicier than most.

I remember getting my hair trimmed about two days after one of our gatherings. The woman cutting my hair was more than a little distracted. Finally, she abruptly stopped in her efforts, stepped back and said she couldn't endure the odors that were still emanating from my pores. I suggested some mouthwash. She suggested coming back in a few more days.

Eerily similar approach with the chicken thighs and preparation as the enchiladas. Use that same aluminum oval and prepare the thighs similarly before cooking.

Serves 6 people

2 lbs. boneless, skinless chicken thighs

3 Tbsp olive oil

3 Tbsp chopped fresh ginger

8 cloves, smashed and peeled, coarsely chopped

½ yellow onion finely chopped

¾ cup mango-orange juice, we use "Simply Orange" brand

¼ cup lite soy sauce

4 Tbsp dark brown sugar

3-4 Tbsp curry powder

We buy a medium-colored and spiced variety in bulk. If you want heat, you can step up and start with 1 medium finely-chopped habanero, ½ tsp harissa paste and warn your guests. Double those last 2 ingredients if you're tolerant.

2 Tbsp cream cheese

1. In that oval aluminum roaster, heat the olive oil and add the thighs.

2. Cook 10-12 minutes over medium high heat until thighs start to brown.

3. Add the ginger, garlic and onion...and habanero(s) if used.

4. Continue to cook over same heat, stirring. Don't allow garlic or ginger to brown.

5. In a measuring cup, mix together the juice, soy, and brown sugar, and mix well.

6. Add the juice mixture and curry to the thighs and cook 5 minutes at same heat.

7. Reduce heat to low and simmer for 2 hours. If needed, add some chicken broth, but you want this to cook until it easily shreds apart. Taste and add any additional spices as suits you.

8. Add the cream cheese and mix well. Simmer another 20 minutes until you're happy.

*** We serve Chicken Curry with brussels sprouts ginger/peanut and Thai lime rice from "Buds and Spuds" and beer, of course. An IPA is suggested.

HALLOWEEN CHICKEN

We have some feisty neighbors across the alley from us. Delia is a fine-art sculptor, and welding is her special skill. That same part of the brain carves clever pumpkins, and early on a Halloween Friday evening, Mary was off to check out the illuminated porch art, bottle of Rodney Strong's Cab in hand. I was well into the basics of starting a batch of chicken thighs in the oval. They had been cut in the preferred fashion, slightly browned in olive oil and double-dosed with garlic – enough to deal with werewolves, vampires and lighthouse keepers sure to be out in numbers. I had peeled, seeded and cubed a butternut squash, let it swim in some olive oil seasoned with Italian herbs, sea salt and a bit of sundried tomato pesto, and thrown it into the oven. When my phone rang, it was Mary and Delia's husband Brent, urging me to slither across the alley, imploring me to grab another bottle of red, and join in some pumpkin viewing. Just before racing out the back door, I decided to put about 12 oz. of chardonnay, a little broth and a handful of Herbs de Provence, plus a dash of black sea salt, in with the chicken and lowered the heat, dropping the temp a notch so as not to burn the squash – and then I bolted.

Time does fly when you're having fun, and on occasion takes to great heights before a little alarm sets off. And the thought of my house afire, or worse yet smoke billowing from stove top and oven (and those thighs charred) flashed in my mind. Straight outta there.

Things looked good as I first saw through the kitchen window. No flames. No smoke. Lid off the oval and squash jerked out of oven. My first trick-or-treater. Welcome, little ones, all under control here. Don't put your candy next to the roaring fireplace when you get home! Back to the kitchen. In sports, the Hail Mary, half-court shot at the buzzer and the walk off. Browned, caramelized perfection. Provencal Halloween Chicken served with Arborio Rice and Butternut Squash in "Buds & Spuds," And that is a recipe that must be adhered to strictly.

Chicken Mole

Last recipe using the oval. It goes without saying for this and the last chicken thigh recipe, which is wok-cooked, thighs are cut and scored as usual. If not making home-style mole as prescribed here, I highly recommend a prepared version from Cultura Chocolate. You will find other amazing delights from these fanciers.

2 lbs. boneless, skinless chicken thighs

4 Tbsp of lard or olive oil

1 cup chicken broth

5 ancho chiles, stems, seeds and veins removed

5 guajillo chiles, stems, seeds and veins removed

2 yellow onions, coarsely chopped

6 garlic cloves

1 15 oz. fire-roasted, crushed tomatoes (Muir Valley suggested)

1 tsp cloves

1 tsp coriander

1 Tbsp cinnamon

2 oz. dark unsweetened chocolate (Cultura is best in US.) Try with chiles added.

Brown the chicken thighs in olive oil/lard as per usual until browned and set aside. **1**

Soak the anchos and guajillo chiles in 1 ½ cup of hot water until soft. Remove seeds and stems and save liquid. **2**

In a blender/Cuisinart fitted with a steel blade, blend chiles and half the liquid, onions, garlic, tomatoes, cloves, coriander, cinnamon and chocolate. **3**

Add mixture to chicken and simmer at low heat for 1 hour until thickened. Use chicken broth to keep at the desired thickness for the mole. **4**

Marinated Stir Fried Chicken Thighs

Serves 6 people

2 lbs. boneless, skinless chicken thighs, cut and scored as usual, the flatter the better

3 Tbsp peanut oil

Marinade:

3 Tbsp Shao Hsing wine or fish sauce

3 Tbsp sesame oil

3 Tbsp lite soy

1 Tbsp Sriracha with garlic

2 Tbsp fresh ginger, minced

1 bunch scallions, chopped, green part included

1 mango, peeled, seeded and mashed

½ cup, coarse brown sugar

1 Thoroughly mix all marinade ingredients in a bowl large enough to soak those thighs for 2 hrs.

2 Fry the thighs in the wok in peanut oil, turning often until golden brown and remove, set aside.

3 Add the marinade to the wok and reduce the liquid on medium high for 5-7 minutes until it thickens to a syrup.

4 Return the thighs for a hot bath in the marinade for 2 minutes and serve.

CHICKEN BREAST CUTLETS

We like to use evenly thin cutlets for our recipes. Learn to do it yourself with a sharp knife and tenderize by pounding flat, which is best accomplished using a mallet with the chicken pieces inside a plastic grocery bag. (One of the most useful ways to use those damn things – other uses being for disposing of shrimp shells, salmon skins and other such.) Or buy Perdue's. Never overcook chicken in this way. Serve elegantly tender.

We'll forgo some of our mainstays, such as Marsala and Piccata because our twists on these just don't merit it. We'll share a few that are classics, but therein we wander to the road less traveled.

Chicken Parmesan

Serves 4 people

8 chicken cutlets roughly 5" X 5" if they were square

1 egg well beaten in a flat bowl

1 cup Italian bread crumbs

4-5 Tbsp olive oil

1 ½ cup marinara

5 Tbsp sun-dried tomato pesto

5 Tbsp basil pesto

3 Tbsp Italian herbs

½ cup coarsely shaved Parmesan

½ cup shaved Pecorino regianno

½ cup shredded mozzarella

1 Fry 4 cutlets in the olive oil at a time, after washing in the egg and coating with breadcrumbs. Very important to use a skillet large enough to fry 4 at a time until light golden brown, only 2-3 minutes a side. Then place in a large Pyrex baking dish spread with 1 cup marinara.

2 Continue with the last 4 cutlets and place in baking dish. Don't layer the chicken.

3 Use a spoon to evenly coat the cutlets with both pestos.

4 Next, evenly distribute the 3 cheeses over the cutlets.

5 Sprinkle the herbs over the top.

6 Cover with foil and bake in a preheated oven at 375 for 15 minutes. Remove foil and bake another 5-7 minutes until things are bubbly and turning light golden.

7 This can be served up to 15 minutes after removed from oven.

Chicken Cutlets with Pears

Serves 4 people

8 chicken cutlets as you used for the Chicken Parmesan recipe

1 egg, well beaten in a flat bowl

Flour for dredging, not breadcrumbs

3 pears (bartlett and anjou both work), peeled, stem removed and sliced thin

4-5 Tbsp butter

2 Tbsp of pear preserves or chutney

1 shot of brandy

½ cup chicken broth

1 tsp cinnamon

1 Tbsp brown sugar or to taste

Sea salt and coarse black pepper to taste

1 Melt half the butter in a skillet big enough to sauté the pears, add the preserves and half the broth and cook for a few minutes over medium heat.

2 Add the brandy and simmer for 2-3 more minutes, flare off the brandy if you wish.

3 Add the pears and sauté uncovered for 5 minutes stirring all together well. Add the brown sugar, remaining broth, cinnamon and sugar. Mix well and simmer covered at medium low heat until pears are cooked but not browned. Remove from heat and keep covered. This mixture should have thickened nicely.

4 Fry the cutlets in butter after the egg wash and coating with flour in a skillet at medium high, 4 at a time until lightly browned on both sides. Repeat with the remaining cutlets using enough butter to suit and plate the cutlets. Cover the chicken with the pear mixture proportionally and serve.

Grilled Chicken Breast with Peaches

We first came across this recipe in one of our newspapers about ten years ago. If you lived in a state where peaches were a big deal and a pride crop, it was easy to dive into what seemed, at the time, to be risky business. But we relied on our peaches, not our skill. Now the food world has crisscrossed this idea in numerous ways. This is how we have narrowed this popular preparation down. Grilling large bone-in chicken breasts isn't that hard if you follow a few key steps. Neither is finding fabulous peaches in our home state throughout August. This is not a recommended entree for February. Get freaky in late summertime. This serves 4 people, but we have doubled it many times for a pot that had more names in it.

4 large bone-in chicken breasts, rubbed with salt and pepper at room temperature and set aside in a glass bowl

7 oz. quality peach preserves

2 Tbsp lite soy sauce

2 Tbsp Dijon mustard

3 cloves garlic, peeled and crushed

2 jalapeños, stem removed, halved and seeds removed and coarsely chopped

4 peaches, halved and pit removed, then quartered

4 ounces of Grand Marnier and Peach Brandy

In a food processor or blender fitted with a steel blade, puree **1** the 7 oz. peach preserves, soy, mustard, garlic and jalapeños.

Add half the blended mixture to the chicken breasts for 1 hour **2** at room temperature.

Prepare the peaches and have a shot of Grand Marnier with **3** your guests.

Get the grill set by having half the surface at 375 degrees direct **4** heat and the other half indirect heat only.

Here is where the fun begins. It's easy. Place the marinated **5** breasts bone side down on the indirect heat and grill for 20 minutes, then flip and grill skin side down for 10 minutes. If you have a meat thermometer, check that the breasts are 140 degrees in the center or semi-firm to the touch.

Place the breasts bone side down and, using a brush, coat the **6** skin with the preserve marinade and grill over the direct heat for 5 minutes. If inclined, have another shot of Grand Marnier.

Time to grill the peaches over the indirect heat, mindfully **7** protecting those fruits from overcooking. A turn or two is next.

Now go nuts and baste both the chicken and peaches as you **8** please with the remaining marinade, peach preserves and brandy, and grill another 3-5 minutes. It will be perfect.

PORKIN AWAY IN THE KITCHEN

Pig. More parts therein and interesting ways to prepare oinkers than any protein I can think of. Whole cooked in the ground overnight, mo-shu-ro, dumplings, brined and slow cooked shank, tacos al pastor, Virginia cured ham, Cuban sandwiches, braised stuffed chops with herb dressing, Italian sausage 20 ways, pancetta, eggs Benedict with Canadian bacon, bacon, ribs, pan fried tenderloin, adobo, boneless Italian roasts, breakfast sausage, bratwurst, sweet and sour, ham hocks, jambalaya, chorizo, chicharonnes, salami, salami, bologna!

Pan Fried Pork Tenderloin

The best way we've found to cook these are pan fried in a mix of olive oil and butter over medium high heat for about 7-8 minutes a side after seasoning. A light medium-cooked center will retain the moisture and texture best. Cooking times vary, based on diameter. Marinating in Green River Sauce and grilling, coating with basil pesto and oven cooking have all worked, but try this method and it may convert you. There are such a variety of sauces, jams, preserves and toppings to use as finishes that these tenderloins find our table almost every week. We'll run down the frying method and suggest a few favorite rubs and finishes. The ones we buy run about 1 ¼ lb. to 1 ½ lb. which I suggest for 2 people. A pork sandwich Cuban style is great for lunch a day or two later.

Season meat with a mix of lemon pepper, sea salt, black pepper, garlic powder and cayenne, the basic rub. Heat the olive oil and butter in that good skillet until hot but not smoking hot. Fry the meat as suggested and attend to it by cooking on all sides and cover partially when not turning. Total cooking time will vary from 12 to 20 minutes until you get used to the temperature of the stovetop and the desired wellness of the meat. I actually prefer medium rare, while your preference may be burnt. Remove from the heat and slice to your desired thickness and serve. Have your Buds and Spuds and finishes ready to go.

Some rubs: Olive oil, then roll in Herbs de Provence, black sea salt, coarse black pepper, and a mix of paprika, salt, garlic & onion powders.

Finishes: All are savory reductions of fruit preserves or jams. We're lucky each year to receive a care package of incredible goods from Sally's kitchen, pear-apricot chutney, plum chutney, bacon jam. But in the stores you can find ginger spread, apricot preserves, black currant preserves and a lot of others. Here's one of my originals that is also well suited for wild duck or woodcock:

Melt 3 Tbsp butter, add 32 cloves chopped garlic (ha!), 2 Tbsp red currant jelly, juice of 1 fresh lemon, 1 Tbsp of Lea and Perrin's and reduce.

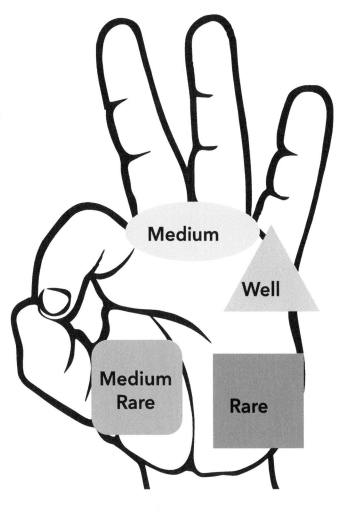

*Meat Thermometer

Pork Green Chili

I live in a town where this is more hotly debated than politics or the weather. Just a note about the use of chilies. They vary like your taste. Make sure you and yours are tolerant and then enjoy. Start mild and add hotter chilies if desired. Harrisa paste is just a mixture of a little olive oil, chilies and cumin. I buy mine prepared from the best. Here's mine.

1 ½ lb. pork tenderloin cubed

1 lb. pork country rib meat cubed

4 Tbsp olive oil

10 cloves coarsely chopped garlic

6 anaheim chilies, roasted, peeled, seeded and chopped – or if you live in a town like mine, on the roadsides or at farmer's markets, buy the quart-sized bags of fresh roasted Hatch Chilies. Some roasters are even kind enough to label them, mild, medium or hot.

1 ½ cup lo-so chicken broth

1 15 oz. can Stokes's Green Chili with Pork (optional) but a smart addition for some

1 Tbsp Harrisa paste (optional)

1 Tbsp ground cumin

1 Tbsp sea salt

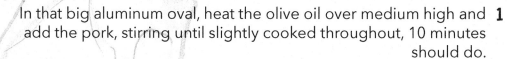

1 In that big aluminum oval, heat the olive oil over medium high and add the pork, stirring until slightly cooked throughout, 10 minutes should do.

2 Add the garlic and continue to stir for 5 minutes. Add the broth, green chilies, Stoke's, Harrisa paste, cumin and sea salt.

3 Stir ingredients for 5-7 minutes at this temperature, reduce heat to low and simmer for 2 hours.

4 Uncover occasionally and simmer and fine tune the spices to your preference. After your second go round, you will have your own original.

Carnitas

Some abuelas from Sonora, LA, or San Antonio would be rather dismayed and probably horrified making carnitas this way. No argument there. When you find them done right in that old way, they are sublime. Simple is better in most cases. But here is Mary's version, which has a strong following. They are bright, piquant and savory. Wonderful and easy to prepare.

4 lb. pork shoulder roast, bone in and cut into about 8 evenly sized pieces

4-6 Tbsp olive oil or lard

8 garlic cloves, smashed and coarsely chopped

1 large yellow onion, coarsely chopped

Chicken broth

1 ½ cup orange – mango juice

2 chili powders, a dark ancho variety and a spicy New Mexico

2 Tbsp ground cumin

Cinnamon

Fresh corn and flour tortillas

Chopped fresh mango, sliced avocados, coarsely chopped fresh cilantro and sour cream as condiments

1 Brown the pork in the olive oil in a big oval aluminum roaster at medium high heat on the stovetop. This will take at least 10 minutes to get it right.

2 Add the garlic and onion, continue to stir avoid burning the garlic.

3 Add chicken broth and juice to about half way to the top of the pork. Add chili powders, cumin and cinnamon if desired. This is funny because I asked Mary to tell me about what portions she uses for the spices. She just said, "You know, however much you need to get it right." A cook's answer. We want to slow simmer, not boil for 2 ½ - 3 hours. Pork should shred easily.

4 Serve with warm fresh tortillas and the other condiments.

Vicki's Baby Backs

Struggled most of my life trying to get this right. This is where I've landed. Low and slow. Whether St. Louis style, baby backs or country style this will work. I prepare baby back as a preference. I don't own Eddy's smoker but that is a great alternate...and his sauce.

Serves 6-8 people

3 full racks of baby backs. About 13 -14 bones each, depending how they're cut

Sea salt and coarse black pepper to taste

4 Tbsp BBQ rub or Cajun seasoning

1 Remove the membrane from the inside of the racks. This is a technique you need to try: Start lifting the membrane from one end with a small sharp knife. Use a paper towel and, in one shot, peel that membrane away and discard. Cut the ribs as pairs. 2-rib sets.

2 Rub the ribs with BBQ rub, salt and pepper and place in a large oven roasting pan. Add enough water to a ½" level, cover tightly with aluminum foil. Bake at 225 degrees for 4 hours. Convection ovens, same temp for 3 hours. Make sure there is always enough liquid. Steam, don't boil or cook dry. The ribs should be falling off the bone when done.

3 Finish the ribs on a grill after liberally brushing with sauce at 375-400 degrees to suit. Everyone has their preference. I suggest some be blackened, others not.

Eddy's Version:

Eddy is a master. A cook's cook. Plying a recipe out of him is pulling teeth. "Well you know, I use some of this and that, you mix some of this and taste it and.........." Ed cooks his ribs in a smoker at low temp. His method is to do a rub, coat the ribs (he cooks all three cuts together, country, St. Louis style and baby backs in foil for 4 hours at 250 degrees. Open the packets, add apple juice and smoke again for 30 minutes. Then he sets them free and finishes them for twenty minutes basting with a modest amount of his BBQ sauce.

Secrets divulged. The rub as best as can be translated:

Kosher Salt, oregano, paprika, cumin, dry mustard, garlic powder, chili powder, brown sugar and Saigon cinnamon.

The Sauce:

2 cups each of Jack Daniels Bourbon and ketchup. Lea & Perrins, molasses, sautéed onions and red pepper flakes. And there you have it.

NO IRISH POPE?
PART 2 THE WEDDING

FRIDAY MORNING AND STILL at the Fitzgerald's. NNow awake and time to take stock. My "sleep" that was oft interrupted by awakening was most strange. My brain relied on dreaming in a suspended state, as I hovered over my dreams from above like a dragonfly repeating its flight pattern at a twenty-foot distance. First, there was a uniformed Aer Lingus stewardess handing out little bags of potato chips from a wicker basket to a line of American Cub Scouts in proper blue attire, all near the gas pumps in front of the Fitzgerald business. Then there was an eel the size of an Amazon python that emerged from the waterway and crossed Mossie's handiwork in the concrete slab, heading for our quarters.

I came to the conclusion that this was not going to be a day filled with fun and frolic with my new acquaintance, Mossie Fitz. There would be no morning passing the football in the yard or an afternoon excursion to the pubs to be introduced to his mates, "This is James Duffey, American Asshole Supreme. Let's all welcome him to Ireland and raise a pint in his name!" With Mrs. Fitz at the helm there was the likelihood that I would be rescued and be involved with the ladies planning for the big day tomorrow.

I don't recall much of that Friday morning, but about noon it was time to hit the road with the gals, and I deferred to sit in the back again while the women in the front were nice enough to inform me of the various stops that lay ahead: first the church, then the hall where the reception would be held to review details with the proprietor, then to a clothier for some stitch-ups and, finally, back to the church for a rehearsal of the wedding. Sheila seemed particularly animated and very talkative. She asked how my sleep was and I chuckled a bit and told her about the stewardess dream. I was corrected in that the chips being given out were called "crisps" in Ireland and that chips were sold everywhere, but most notably with fried fish at a "Chippie." I'm certain that I would never have remembered those dreams were it not for this new vocabulary lesson. I drifted a moment, thinking about how there were a handful of dreams that recurred in my childhood that have never been forgotten, one of which started when I was about four or five years old. It involved the villain Yosemite Sam, nemesis to Bugs Bunny, who would come at night to our back porch and try to abduct me. Scary as hell. I dreamt that time and again. Television was powerful and so were the images that got lodged in a young boy's mind.

"Are you going to sing a song for us at tomorrow's wedding reception, James?" Mrs. Fitz suddenly asked. I was only slightly staggered, unlike a full blow to the head, and quickly responded, "Of course, love to." Jesus, Mary and Joseph. I do not sing well. And what the hell would I sing. Sheila now started a lively discussion of the current music world. For those of my genre, music was a preeminent issue – discussing music was an important social currency, and there were no borders. We all had radio and vinyl, plus a few 8-tracks, so this was always an exciting topic. I knew stuff and liked artists that were from a wide landscape. I loved the roots of American jazz and blues that formed the rock and roll world of Great Britain and the US...and Ireland. I was also a smug SOB. Sheila shelled me with inquiries, and I realized she was no slouch either. She lived in San Francisco, was well-versed and loved music. Motown, Thin Lizzy, Donovan Leitch, John Mayall and the Blues Breakers, Cream, Blind Faith, Three Dog Night, the Dead, Starship, Jackson Five, Muddy Waters, Coltrane, Miles Davis, even Walter Johnson and Junior Wells – she knew them all. No bullshitting this lass. "Ever heard of Cory Gallagher?" she inquired.

"Nope, never heard him."

"I love him, like him as much as Jimi Hendrix. You will too if you hear him. An Irishman." That was bold. And a thrashing.

I asked, "Ever heard of Leonard Cohen?"

"Of course," she responded. "I love his stuff, he's a Canadian."

Christ, I hope I can remember the words.

On our appointed rounds, I was moved by the landscape, the rolling hills and their greenery. The roads were very narrow in parts, with some never intended to be driven on, what with the stone walls placed so close to the traffic lane that oncoming cars had to be met with caution. Add to this the frequent livestock ranging to and fro and the farmers and their carts mixing in. Speeding would have been ill advised. Sheila affectionately referred to some of the gents wheeling along as "paddys" but pointed out that there were less flattering names used by some. I had never spent time in a "third world" country, but I was close.

Sitting in the church in the late afternoon on this sunny day with light filtering in through the stained glass windows, making a soft golden backdrop while a priest reviewed the details of how to get hitched, Catholic style, was a pleasure. In twenty-four hours we would be elsewhere merrymaking, boisterously celebrating and listening to some take the microphone.

Saturday morning arrived bathed in the same golden glow as the previous dusk. Things were happening already in the Fitz compound. All were up and I could hear the lively conversation and associated clatter coming from headquarters. I had to take stock for a moment and think about the contents of that Navy duffel. Was I prepared for a wedding? I stopped cold for a moment and reflected on the bag itself and its contents. It was, in itself, and most of its tightly folded and compressed tenants were, the result of my life benefactor, my brother-in-law Steve. He didn't underwrite my escapades but he endorsed them. Without judgment and with love. He was the light in the dark tunnel, even right now, when, if it would have been possible to tell him where I was and what was going on, he would have laughed. God, I missed him.

Prepsterhood was about to pay great dividends. In addition to my herringbone tweed worn since leaving my status as

visitor and migrant farmer in Princeton, there was a nice houndstooth jacket, two rolled up button-down oxfords, two pairs of khaki slacks appropriately over-sized in the cuff, baggy and intentionally short, and the L.L. Bean Blucher Moccasins, never tied. Socks? Shite, yes, I was actually thinking back a few and had two pairs of rag socks. The final touch that was rolled up into the sleeve of that natty houndstooth was a beautiful maroon paisley tie, gratis, of course, from Steve. I was set, regardless of being unpressed, another prerequisite of mine. I assembled my armor and decided I was fit for anything. This was attire for any great event, whether love, battle or war.

After the offering and acceptance of nourishment, there was an assembly of sorts. Who was driving with whom to where and when and – thinking forward past the wedding to the reception and then on to an unnamed pub in the countryside some distance from the reception hall – we all anticipated the next stage, convivial dancing and general partying. As usual, Mrs. Fitz was sergeant and I followed her recommendations. After driving with Big Sis and Mossie we were to meet outside the church, a twenty-minute drive in some direction to which I already had lost all coordinates. Splendid. I would never need to know my whereabouts or how to collect my belongings in the event I went wayward. Just the way I liked it. I was being escorted.

Having arrived at the church, my escorts were greeted by many familiar to them. I was introduced to very few until the main crew arrived from the Fitz's household. Sheila grabbed my elbow and introduced me to cousins, aunties, neighbors and such whom I had been milling around with but not had the joy of introduction. I heard one auntie say to the other, "He looks Italian, not Irish," and that was with a little scorn. That's right, a frigging Guinea Hen has invaded the event, American as well. Yup. Next up, a Negro, followed by a Puerto Rican. I wasn't weary, just still a little off from my two full days abroad. So

many hellos and hugs. Hugs and hellos.

It was nearing time to enter the church and witness one of the seven Blessed Sacraments of Matrimony. I've been baptized, took my first Holy Eucharist, been confirmed, given penance, (sure as hell was not going to be ordained), and married most likely someday, but the last I saw administered once, the Extreme Unction, for which I'll take a permanent pass.

As people started to enter church, I was certain that I'd find a pew in the rear to nestle in and watch the proceedings from afar. Easier positioning to go unnoticed, as I had lost my fondness for all of the successions of kneeling, standing and sitting associated with a Catholic Mass. Of course that was nixed, as Mrs. Fitz found me and insisted that I sit up front with the immediate family – and there I was, front row. A displaced dignitary.

The wedding went off much like the five previous ones I had witnessed, all in a Catholic church. The usual smells and bells and drawn out combo shot of Mass and Matrimony. During the M&M I reflected about The Church. It had played a big role in my formative years. I was now older and decided to use this time to reflect – fear, guilt, discovery, rebellion and literacy. A toss-up.

People were gathered to join the newlyweds in front of the church. Another sunny mid-day in Ireland. Always a time of great expectations when these couples greet the world in their new status, and this one appeared to be an expression of true love. I was only thinking about what lay ahead, however: I had a performance to prepare for and, for the first time, heard of a later gathering that many were sure to attend at a public roadhouse. It was in the countryside somewhere between the reception's location and the Irish Sea.

It was a first time ride with women the only, sans Mrs. Fitz. Lots of chatter with a large amount of slagging. I was a bit

anxious and rolled down my window surreptitiously. My pending performance was weighing on my mind. And so was the recent past. Out of diplomacy, I had received the Eucharist. It had been nearly five years since I gave my penance. Jesus, Mary and Joseph. The sins were piling up. That could be considered another mortal sin.

"Father, it has been nearly five years since my last confession; these are my sins. I suggest you reach down and take a serious pull on that jug because there has been a lot of water gone under the bridge. In fact, there are many things floating in that water. I have a spreadsheet I've prepared by violation and degree of impurity that you should review. If you need a week or two to review and get back with me, don't hesitate."

I had deemed that "Suzanne" by Leonard Cohen would be the song I would perform for my Irish stage debut. I was going through the lyrics in my head. Yikes! "Jesus was a sailor when he walked upon the water... He himself was broken long before the sky would open, forsaken, almost human, He sank before your wisdom like a stone." I was soon to commit blasphemy! Was this gravely immoral like drunkenness and reveling as the catechism had taught? Or a drop-down offense, a Catholic misdemeanor of the venial variety? Hell, why worry. I'd mumble my way through that verse and trust the revelers were too boisterous to pay close attention. Or perhaps there would be some amnesia by Sheila and Mrs. Fitz.

A lively assembly of all ages greeted the newlyweds at the reception hall. Children, grannies, aunts, uncles, neighbors, clergy, Mossie and his crew, and a lone American entered a hall with a sizable stage already occupied by musicians. A feast awaited all after the greetings were complete. This event had charm. And there were was no small amount of protocol that had to be followed for this to be a proper event, as well as charming one. A prayer by the ordained in attendance, toasts, kissing by the bride and groom (countlessly), the sit-down

dinner between Sheila and her sister, dancing pairs of all varieties, and a modest but continuous consumption of stouts and ales. Things would soon start to ramp up.

A middle-aged man was the first to charm the crowd with a rendition of an Irish melody. He was followed by two female performances. Every song was so charming and poised. They had practiced. I left the hall to join a group outside that were smoking cigarettes. I didn't smoke but held my pint and joined in only when directly addressed. "No, not Chicago, but close. Met Sheila only two days ago. Would stay in Ireland as long as my money would last. Played sports and liked to drink beer and dance with girls. No thanks, cigs make me dizzy."

Returning to the hall, I saw Sheila signaling me to come to her. "You're going to sing next after my sister's father-in-law.

I love "Suzanne." But I was hoping for a catastrophe. Perhaps a power failure or someone would have an untimely and unfortunate seizure or Mossie and crew would disrupt my debut. Those damn lyrics. Empowered by a few pints of Guinness, though, I was in queue. My thespian career as a prepster had me prepared in one way – I did not suffer from stage fright. In fact, I suffered from an unusual confidence in front of a crowd. The band knew the song vaguely and said they would strum a few likely chords but it was my show. They didn't have a libretto or a clue.

My range and skills as a singer were poor. I had grown up in a family with sisters who sang like angels and a brother who had a great sense of rhythm. I had none of these. If I had learned anything in the last two days it was that these Irish people were the most generous, open-hearted folks I had ever met. My rendition was dreadful. Yet there was polite applause and words of encouragement. If I hadn't obliged Sheila with my pledge to sing, I would have offered to officiate a lady's smock race or refereed a sparring match between Mossie and Jack Dempsey.

In the early dusk, people filtered out of the reception hall and there was quite a bit of talk about the day's Main Event. Most were all heading to a roadhouse. Bar time was 11:00 PM but on Saturday night, rules were slightly more lenient with an extra half hour allowed for "drink-up time." The joint had live music and allowed dancing. In the past two days as a passenger I had driven by many public houses that were what I had envisioned – small, inviting, inns with traditional signage that looked like they had grown out of the Irish soil like indigenous trees.

We arrived after dark and the joint looked like it could be displaced from Mississippi or Wisconsin. Large gravel parking lot on the side and in the rear, both well-lit, no distinguishing signage or aplomb. The interior was vast and primarily fitted with picnic tables that sat about ten each.

Our table was crowded and a bit raucous. Sheila and I had only experienced a brief hand touch a couple of days earlier. We had a dance or two and were finally getting just a little frisky, but still totally appropriate. Walking off the dance floor arm and arm and a brief hug – those were our limits. We found our place at the table. Whatever happened next has no clear explanation. A thud would be descriptive, followed by some brief time to take stock. I did not lose complete consciousness but recalled the same feeling I had experienced falling out of bed and landing on my head. I was on the floor having apparently been laid out with a hook from a fist. As I looked up, there was Mossie atop the damn table. He was uttering, "You won't mickey my sister." Never heard that expression before but I did not need a translator. He had either suckered me with a hook or, according to another's comment, gave my noggin a drop kick. Sheila showed a bit of concern but everybody else was thrilled, and when the barman showed up to appraise the scene, he said, "Take it out back boys, lots of room back there and good lighting as well." Just the support I was looking for.

A crowd of about fifty people formed a ring in the rear parking lot with most cheering on Mossie to kick my ass. I was never fond of the thought of slamming my bare knuckles into another man's face, nor did I relish being hit in the same way. My pugilistic instinct was to whack him in the side of his face with an open hand. Bingo! Point to the American. What ensued would never have been referred to as the "Sweet Science." Things deteriorated into a wrestling match that would best be described as two bear cubs flailing harmlessly. Our non-paying audience was wanting more action and Mossie was intent on delivering. My senses were just slightly more acute as he took a wild swing at me that I backed away from, but put him in a precariously off-balanced position. So I wrestled him to the ground where we rolled around and around in the gravel. After securing a slight advantage by resting on top of him, things came to an abrupt halt. Some of the older patrons were alarmed and had the barmen call the garda. I was pulled away from my pal by the barman and firmly escorted toward the lighted side of the roadhouse. This was a wise and witful man in his middle age. And powerful. "There will be no trouble for ya if you just leave. I'll talk with the garda and explain. But don't stick around, even for a minute after they arrive. Do as they say."

Sure enough, the uniformed arrived. I thought that this was probably a usual stop in their Saturday night travels through the dark countryside to disperse the drink-up time crowd and restore any order that had been disrupted. The two men were not as cordial as the barman, but straightforward and as wise. "You have to leave, lad. Where are you staying?" I pointed out into the dark and told them it was a toss-up. To the right or the left. "I am rudderless, officers. I have to get back to a family's house to collect my things. Their name is Fitzgerald and they have gas pumps and a nice house."

"Don't know where that is, but get a move on before there is

more trouble."

Forging on. The front of the joint was dark where it met the road. I looked both ways into the absolute darkness of the Irish countryside. Decided without any rationale I would start walking to the right, no compass, the other point was left. I would thumb it, hoping for some distant lights to arrive before the pub crowd emerged. My mind was frazzled but I thought I saw a very dim light coming my direction. It seemed interminable for this light to come into focus, but it was heading my direction! If it was a car and capable of carrying another passenger, no gesture of my distress was ruled out. I could now make out two headlights moving closer and closer. Damn. The car looked the size of a soapbox derby entrant. I waved my arms frantically and exaggerated the hitchhiking motion, thumb swinging from my ankles to over my head. They stopped after initially passing me by, and now the car was backing up wildly. Music was blaring and the two male inhabitants stopped just short of amputating my right leg. "Hop in mate."

My saviors were guttered, completely cabbaged. After squeezing myself into the back seat and trying to find a way to sit sideways across it, I was passed the bottle of Paddy's. "Looks like you could use this, mate. Dunno where you going but if it's past my ma and da's farm, you can stay in the barn and move on in the morn."

"Trying to find a place called Fitzgeralds. Don't know where it's at."

My boys, in their early twenties, I surmised, just laughed. "You're a damned Yank and look like shite, and don't know where you're going? Ya got yourself in a fight with another lad. Do you like Muhammad Ali?"

"Can I have another notch from that piss?"

"All you want, we have more in the barn."

Perfect. No clue where I was heading and removed from any belongings. Going to slam whisky in a barn, without any assurances of reuniting with my Naval bag. Ever.

BEEF, IT'S WHATS FOR DINNER UNLESS YOU CAN BARTER FOR SOME ELK

Whatever we prepare with beef, the best cuts and sources are what we use. It's not something as part of a daily diet, so when you're in the mood for beef, buy the best...or barter for elk.

Beef Stew

For 6 people

2 ½ lb. beef chuck boneless pot roast, cut into 1 ½" pieces

1 cup flour to dredge

¼ cup olive oil

1 large onion chopped

8-10 garlic cloves coarsely chopped

15 oz. can consommé

6 oz. can tomato paste

1 ½ cup red wine (a sweet blend is my suggestion)

3 Tbsp Herbes de Provence

Coarse sea salt and black pepper to taste

Low sodium beef broth (or more wine) as needed

1 lb. carrots cut into ½" slices

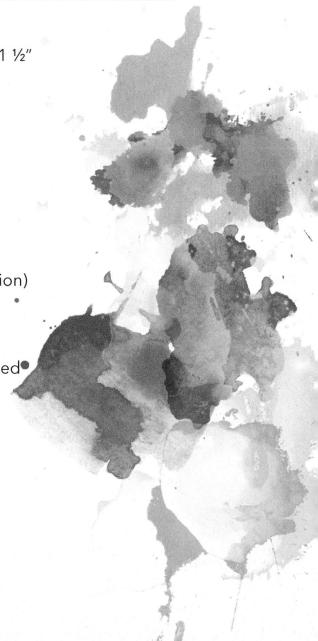

1 In that stove top aluminum oval, heat the olive oil and add the dredged beef,

2 Brown for 7-10 minutes over medium high heat, add onion and garlic, and continue to sauté but don't burn any ingredients.

3 Add consommé, tomato paste, red wine, herbs and continue to stir. Continue to cook at medium high and stir. Add salt and pepper sparingly to start and simmer covered on low heat for 2 hours.

4 Make sure to not let beef stick to the bottom of the pan to avoid risk of burning any ingredient. Cover intermittently.

5 Add broth/wine to your taste and in a volume to give you a modest thickness to the liquid.

6 Add carrots and stir, return to simmer, covered.

7 Cook until beef is tender and season with sea salt and pepper to your taste.

Mashed potatoes and sautéed brussel sprouts are great buds and spuds to accompany.

Beef Machaca

We first had this on a Mother's Day morning in the Baja. It was served with eggs in a twist called Machado con Huevos. That beef was slow cooked and shredded. We've changed things up a bit. This is ideal for that deal you made for some elk.

For 6 people

2 lbs. Thinly sliced top round steak

Here's the rub...mix together in a bowl:

2 Tbsp dried dark chili powder

2 Tbsp dried medium chili powder

2 Tbsp dried Mexican oregano

1 tsp ea. onion and garlic powder

1 tsp cinnamon

1 tsp salt

3 Tbsp olive oil

1 yellow onion, finely chopped

6 garlic cloves, finely chopped

2 medium jalapeños, seeded and finely chopped

12 tortillas, fresh mix of corn and flour

Sour cream, chopped mango, chopped fresh cilantro,

fresh Salsa Cruda

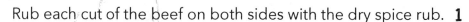

Rub each cut of the beef on both sides with the dry spice rub. **1**

Sauté the beef in your best fry pan in 2 Tbsp of the olive **2** oil on medium high for about 2-3 minutes per side or until nicely browned. Remove beef from skillet and chop into small pieces with a cleaver and set aside. Leave the pan as-is with residue from the sauté.

Add last Tbsp of olive oil to pan and sauté onion, garlic and **3** jalapeno until the mixture starts to brown and then add the chopped beef and fry to your liking... Machaca!

Serve with condiments and tortillas. Strongly suggest our **4** Mexican Rice from buds and spuds.

Baked Whole Tenderloin

This one has become a holiday favorite. It was a hand-me-down from our friend Jimmy (aka Ernesto). We used to serve this to a large crowd at our annual holiday parties, and I cannot think of a single recipe that I have been asked to provide more than this. It will raise some eyebrows for sure, so bet on it. Save your pennies and quarters, as this can be costly if you plan on serving a throng. Count on a 5-6 lb. tenderloin per 10 people. Here you go:

1 whole beef tenderloin trimmed of all membrane and most fat

ketchup

3 Tbsp coarsely ground black peppercorns per tenderloin

plenty of quality Herbs Provence

sea salt to taste

Completely coat the meat generously in ketchup. **1**

Coat this messy loin with herbs and pepper and refrigerate **2** for 1 hour in a rectangular roasting pan.

Preheat the oven to 500 degrees. **3**

Cook the beef uncovered for 20 - 25 minutes. **4**

Some good monitoring at this point is critical to make sure **5** the butt end is rare, the center is medium rare, and the tapered end is medium. Slice into ½" thick pieces

Pappardelle with Bolognese

I first made this with my beloved brother-in-law Steve. It was a maiden voyage into a way of making a spaghetti sauce like neither of us had ever ventured. There was a recipe in one of his many cookbooks that intrigued. Of course, we strayed from the recipe as prescribed, and this is what it has evolved into 40 years later. Remember the axiom that small bits go best with wider al dente pasta and large bites pair best with thin spaghetti.

For 6 people

1 lb. 85% lean ground beef

1 lb. bulk Italian sausage, hot or mild

4-6 garlic cloves coarsely chopped

2 Tbsp sun-dried tomato pesto

2 Tbsp marinara

5 oz. beef consommé

½ cup heavy cream or non-fat Half and Half

1 Tbsp ground nutmeg or to taste

Sea salt to taste

12 oz. package of Al Dente's Pappardelle pasta (a plug for that company)

Plenty of shaved aged Parmesan cheese or asiago (or both)

1 In a skillet large enough to fit all these ingredients, brown the ground beef and sausage,   continuously breaking up the meats. Good sausage is hard to bust up, but do your best. Help is on the way…

2 Put the cooked meats into a food processor fitted with a steel blade and mince it for 30 seconds.

3 Don't liquefy, but ground very fine and then back to the skillet.

4 Add the garlic, pesto, marinara, and consommé and sauté for 10 minutes while stirring.

5 Add the cream, nutmeg, and salt to taste. Lower the heat and simmer low for 15 minutes.

6 Put more cream in as necessary to make a thick creamy Bolognese.

7 Prepare the pappardelle as instructed, not overcooked and serve.

Beef Tenderloins

I can't think of any meat eaters who don't rate this high on their list as a favorite. For most, these are some breaks from the norm, but well worth the try. A 2-minute finish on the grill for æsthetics only, as we prefer ours pan fried. They are very tender and easy to monitor with this method.

4 tenderloin steaks, 8-10 oz.

2 Tbsp butter

2 Tbsp olive oil, lighter sautéing variety preferred

Salt-free lemon pepper

Herbs de Provence

Coarse black pepper

Sea salt to taste

Salt the steaks with lemon pepper and black pepper **1**

Generously coat the steaks entirely with some good Herbs **2** de Provence

In that favorite large skillet, melt the butter and oil over **3** medium high heat.

Fry the steaks at about 450 degrees for about 4 minutes **4** per side with the skillet partially covered. This is a great way to monitor the wellness of each steak, regardless of its size and thickness of cut to suit each person's preferences.

Salt to taste **5**

Green River Fire Pit Grilled Top Sirloin or a Piece of Pig if Karsten's Along

Grilling this beast became a great tradition on our annual July fishing and camping trips to a remote area of the Green River in Utah. Over the years many friends and family would make the trek to the high desert, and I was always charged with procuring, marinating and cooking this 5-6 lb. 1 ½" thick cut of the finest sirloin that could be found. My sourcing always came down to the same small family-owned butcher shop. The folks there wanted a week's advance notice to make sure we got the best.

The sirloin was grilled on an open campfire that sprang from a 2-hour roaring blaze until it settled into a bed of coals that was a foot deep and white hot. Pinon gathered in the camping area served as our fuel. We found that pinon was unparalleled for our use. Someone was charged with tending to the russet potatoes wrapped in foil and tossed directly on the coals, and another roasted the corn with husk intact over the grill. It was sublime.

As mentioned, it was always about the cut of meat that was stuck with a fork many times on both sides before resting in 3-4 cups of Green River Sauce, Dip I (Pg. 29), in a large enough plastic container with a lid and refrigerated 3 days until grill time. Grilling this size piece was not a problem over such a high, consistent temperature. It was easy to serve at any degree of wellness by cutting slices at the desired intervals. Same was true for the spuds and sweet corn.

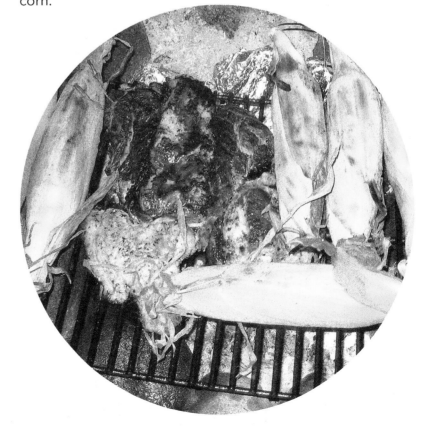

Marinated Lamb Chops

Good French-cut racks of lamb contain about 8 bones and have a nice layer of fat on the outside. This layer of fat is a bit of a mischief, and that is why we always grill them on a hot grill over indirect heat. Do this in your oven broiler one time and you'll understand. Trim about half the fat away before marinating the racks overnight in a shallow glass pan, turning them 3-4 times during the marinating process. Don't overcook. Use Vernes Thermometer as your gauge.

The marinade for 2 racks: Combine the following:

5 oz. olive oil

2 Tbsp red wine vinegar

6-8 garlic cloves, coarsely chopped

2 Tbsp Dijon mustard

1 Tbsp lemon juice

1 Tbsp ginger, fresh minced

1 small yellow onion, sliced thin and cut crosswise

Fresh rosemary and thyme (leaves from 5 sprigs of each)

Grill to suit your tastes. Medium rare is recommended.

BUDS AND SPUDS

Don't look for the exotic in our selections. We suggest how to prepare in the simplest of ways with a variety of twists. Buds and/or spuds should be involved in every meal. Fresh, uncomplicated and savory.

Green Beans

All agree that this is first runner-up. All recipes will be based on a pound of fresh-trimmed, cleaned and dried quality beans. Some cook whole, while others snap in half. Decide your own preference. We'll skip the canned French style, cream of mushroom soup and French fried onion rings sodium crash that we all endured endearingly at Thanksgiving for decades. We will be sautéing and finishing in a variety of ways. Fresh and crisp.

Holiday Style with Sage and Lemon:

Saute in 4 Tbsp. butter for 4-5 minutes over medium high heat, stirring often. Cover on and off. Add zest of 1 large lemon and $1/3$ cup fresh cleaned and chopped sage, continue to sauté for 3-4 minutes. Salt and pepper added to taste. Ready to serve.

A Dazey Way:

Blanch beans snapped in half for 1 minute in hot water and set aside. In a fry pan, saute ½ lb. coarsely chopped pancetta until rendered. Pour off half the fat and add the beans. Sauté until pancetta is browned and beans are still crisp. Add sea salt and pepper to taste. Ready and steady.

An Asian Touch:

Saute in a wok at medium high in 3-4 Tbsp of peanut oil for 3-4 minutes. Add 2 coarsely chopped shallots and 3 cloves of fresh, coarsely chopped garlic, and continue to stir fry for 3 more minutes. Add 1 tsp sugar, 1 Tbsp lite soy and 2 Tbsp sesame oil. Sauté an additional 1-2 minutes and serve. Get freaky and add 1 Tbsp fresh peanut butter when finishing.

Brussels Sprouts

Our King of Buds. All in my crew may not agree what is the best way to "start" the Little Green Balls of Death, but all agree that these finishes are excellent. There are 2 paths that meet at the end, baked at high temp or pan fried. To me, it makes no difference. Choose your method and try each. The finishes herein are from my favorite kitchens.

Prepare sprouts by cutting off the ends and slicing in half lengthwise. The leaves that fall away are a must to save. They become the popcorn equivalents to old maids and superior morsels in the finished recipe. Now comes the crossroads. Some prefer to roast at 425-450 and others sauté at medium high. If you roast, the ingredients should be well mixed in a bowl with the sprouts before baking. If sautéing, you add the finishes at intervals while on the stovetop. Sounds complicated, but don't fall into that trap. This is easy. 1 pound of sprouts for 4 people.

Karsten's

Karsten sautés in olive oil, sea salt, coarsely ground black pepper and a chopped jalapeño until browned and sets aside. In a saucepan, cook the juice of a lime, 1 Tbsp Sriracha, 1 ½ Tbsp honey and add to the buds. Wow.

Kurt's

Kurt sautés in chicken broth until light brown and sets aside. After removing the sprouts he finishes in the same skillet by lightly browning 4-5 shallots finely chopped in butter, 4 Tbsp red wine vinegar and a ½ lb. of coarsely chopped bacon. Mix all ingredients together and sauté to desired color.

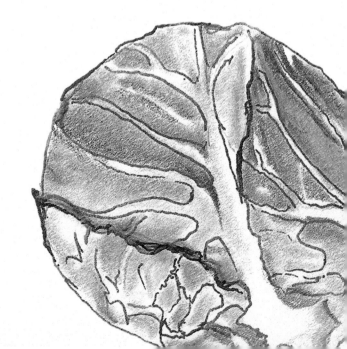

Kaitlin's

Kaitlin fashions her sprouts very uniquely. She cuts 1 lb. of them lengthwise into ⅛" slivers and blanches them in enough chicken broth for 4-5 minutes at medium high until nearly all liquid is evaporated. Then at the same heat, sautés them in olive oil until just slightly browned. To this she adds a preparation of caramelized shallots. This is done by thinly slicing 3 large shallots and adding it to a small frying pan with 3 Tbsp melted butter. Once the shallots are softened and transparent, a Tbsp each of apple cider vinegar and brown sugar are added and cooked until a deep brown and thickened.

Dazey's

Dazey sautés in a combo of olive oil and butter until medium brown, sets aside. In a small saucepan he sautés fresh sage in ¼ lb. of butter and continues until butter is browned. Pours over sprouts and serves.

Mary's

Mary roasts in olive oil, sea salt and coarse black pepper until well browned. Sets aside. In a saucepan sautés 2 Tbsp olive oil, 4-5 Tbsp of peanut sauce and 2 Tbsp shaved fresh ginger until thickened. Combines with sprouts. Phenomenal with Curry Chicken.

Mine

Sautéed like Dazey's. I like darkened brown. In a saucepan sauté ½ lb. fresh chorizo or Italian sausage until browned. Add 1 cup apple juice and reduce. Season with fennel and Italian herbs or Mexican oregano and light chili powder, depending on meat pairing. Combine and sauté together for an additional 5 minutes and serve.

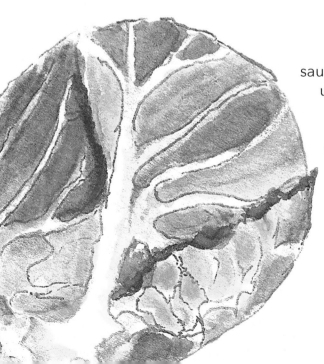

SOME OTHER BUDS

No fear of cooking here. Keeping it crisp. We'll offer some interesting additional bud options.

Stir Fried Snow Peas

Snow Peas should be fresh and very thin. Rinse 1 lb., pinch off the ends and dry thoroughly. Heat 3 Tbsp peanut oil in a wok and sauté at medium high for 3-4 minutes. Add 10-15 thin slices of fresh ginger about the size of a quarter and 1 Tbsp Shao Hsing wine and sauté another minute. Add 1 ½ Tbsp sesame oil, remove from heat and discard the ginger. Serve.

Cole Slaw

A must with Vicki's ribs and all other summer grilling. Add small, cooked shrimp and a good dose of peanut dipping sauce for a light lunch. We use 14 oz. pre-packaged mixes that are a combo of green cabbage, purple cabbage and carrots. Succumb if you're a purist. This stuff is a time and ingredient saver. Grab the bags in the very back. They're 4-5 days fresher. Mix with ¾ cup dressing.

Dressing: Combine ½ cup quality mayonnaise, ¼ cup fresh brewed all natural rice vinegar, coarsely ground black pepper to taste, 2 Tbsp sesame oil (key) and 2 Tbsp dark brown sugar.

Szechuan Broccoli

Karsten calls it nature's broom. We all eat a lot of it. Before the Szechuan style, an easy house favorite is to steam the heads in low sodium chicken broth for 5 minutes, partially covered and still crispy until most of the broth is absorbed. Simply finish with olive oil and lemon pepper. For Szechuan, I like to cut the heads into small pieces about 1 inch in diameter. The stems work also when sliced thin but I don't use them. Makes a great, quick dinner when served with steamed or fried pork dumplings or over scallion pancakes.

1 lb. broccoli

2 Tbsp peanut oil

2 Tbsp minced fresh ginger

2 large garlic cloves coarsely chopped

Mix in a small bowl:

1 Tbsp each of ketchup, lite soy, Shao Hsing wine and garlic chile sauce, 1 tsp sugar, ½ tsp salt and one dried Szechuan red pepper, seeds removed and crushed

Mix 1 tsp cornstarch dissolved in ¼ cup broth and set aside.

1 Stir fry broccoli in the oil for 4-5 minutes at high heat.

2 Add garlic and ginger, stir fry for 1 minute.

3 Add the sauce mixture and continue for 2 minutes, add broth and starch until a nice textured sauce evolves. Serve immediately.

Late Summer Tomatoes

Home grown from a good strain, ate them like apples as a kid with a salt shaker in the other hand. Nothing compares to these at any time of the year wherever sourced. Our favorites are Roma's, grown by my neighbor Terry from seeds given to his wife Betsy from one of her customers where she used to waitress. The story goes these seeds were brought into the mix decades ago from Italy. We are now growing our own from the same seeds, thanks to their largess. Incredible flavor. Here's a spin that extends the magic.

6 medium to large tomatoes, sliced and spread over your serving platter

½ cup finely chopped Italian parsley

⅓ cup extra virgin olive oil

3-4 large garlic cloves, coarsely chopped

1 cup scallions, finely chopped, some green included

¼ cup red wine vinegar

1 Tbsp Dijon mustard

Sea salt and black pepper to taste

1 Mix garlic, onions, parsley, pepper and salt and evenly sprinkle over the sliced tomatoes. Cover and refrigerate 2-3 hours in advance of serving.

2 Combine the olive oil, vinegar and Dijon in a mason jar and mix well and set aside. Pour over tomatoes just before serving.

Eggplant Rollatini

Have to ask for a mandolin slicer as a holiday gift. Worth owning for a lot of preparations. Especially this version of rolatini. Most find this daunting. It is not and will separate you from the pack. Garlic, as Steve noted, protects lighthouse keepers, a savior against werewolves and a must for the gourmets and gourmands.

1 large eggplant with stem cut off, mandolin-sliced thin lengthwise. I use a leather glove when I slice with the mandolin. I like my fingers. Thin enough to wiggle. Lay out on a paper towel and salt. Remove the "sweat" and do the same as other side.

Olive oil as needed to sauté the sliced eggplant

In a bowl mix 1 cup ricotta cheese, 1 Tbsp each of whole fennel seed, Italian spices, 1 egg, ⅓ cup of shaved Parmesan cheese and 3 twists from your sea salt grinder.

1 cup of quality marinara

4 Tbsp each of sundried tomato pesto and garlic basil pesto

½ cup of an Italian cheese blend. Mine has Locatelli and mozzarella.

1 Sauté eggplant in olive oil on both sides until translucent, over medium high and transfer to plate.

2 Spread half the marinara over the bottom of a large Pyrex baking dish.

3 Like rolling a burrito, place about 2 Tbsp of the cheese mixture on each piece of eggplant and roll it up and arrange all in the baking dish.

4 With a spoon evenly spread both pestos over those rolls, then do the same with the remaining marinara and evenly spread the fresh cheeses over all.

5 Bake at 375 F for 15 minutes.

6 Serve with fried or grilled prime Italian sausage links with grilled or roasted red peppers, thin spaghetti and bold red wine.

Peas Nests

Another treat that originally came from Steve and Sally's kitchen as part of holiday fare. Don't know where the recipe originated but now it has morphed into our own holiday addition. Colorful and full of flavor.

1 lb. frozen peas, thawed and blanched in butter and seasoned with nutmeg to taste, about a Tbsp will do. More if you like seasoning with nutmeg and sea salt to taste.

¾ cup cream, heavy or fat-free, your preference

3-4 cloves of garlic, smashed, not chopped

3 Tbsp butter

6 medium carrots cut julienne style, about half the thickness of your pinky finger and as long

2 more Tbsp of butter

1 Tbsp ground cumin

12 slices of wheat bread

Put the blanched and seasoned peas in a blender along with the cream, and **1** puree until smooth. Adjust the flavor with seasonings to your taste. Set aside.

In a saucepan blanch the carrots in enough water to cover for 5-7 minutes **2** over medium heat. Drain the water and add 2 Tbsp butter and the ground cumin. Sauté for 5-7 additional minutes until the carrots are cooked, yet still firm, and set aside.

In a small saucepan at low heat simmer the garlic in 3 Tbsp of butter. What **3** you want is a very flavored butter for brushing on the toast rounds

Toast the bread until medium, cut into rounds about 3" in diameter using a **4** mouth of a glass that width.

To build these nests, place the toast rounds on a cookie sheet big enough **5** to hold all, brush each round with the garlic butter, layer evenly the pea puree on each round and top off with the sautéed carrots on top. Bake at 300 degrees for about 15 minutes until warmed throughout and serve

NO IRISH POPE?
PART 3 THE REVELATION

I WAS APPARENTLY THE FIRST to awake from what was an unsteady sleep. There was a hint of dawn and before I made any motion, I had to take stock. I was contemplating how to liberate some of the Paddy's and Guinness while I assessed my position. I was propped up in a corner of loosely strewn hay in what was an open three-stall garage. My rescuers were sprawled in the same space looking very comfortable.

It took more than a little amount of muster to arise and liberate outside the barn. I had become worried about becoming discovered by a wandering relative looking for his stone markings. "Hello, sir. Yes, I slept in your barn with your valiant offspring. I'm just finishing up a wee and hopping back into my stall until it is proper to be introduced. Cheers!"

Thankfully I settled back into my corner unseen, hoping my rescuers would show a slim sign of life other than the drunken snore. I surveyed my appearance (of what I could see). My khakis, socks and moccasins were a shambles and somewhere my left piece of footwear had become the landlord of a fresh turd. My upper half garments were surprisingly intact, most notably the paisley tie was still well knotted and clean. My sparring partner from the recent Main Event didn't take advantage of what could have been my Achilles. Had he snagged that in his mitts, he might have done some damage.

I decided my best tactic was to stand up and move around our stall and find an object or two to drop within close range of the boys to wake their arses up. I could have just creeped away to the roadside and started afoot, but I trusted that my laddies were my best option to reach my destination. Plus, my compass was still malfunctioning.

It took no time. I had found a rather substantial chain and decided to practice a little American rodeo by using it like a lasso in an attempt to wrap it around one of the upright posts of our stall. Of course, I was unsuccessful and was fortunate not to decapitate me own self, but my men were startled and upright in no time.

"For Chris-sakes, Jimmy, what's going on!"

"Practicing a little rodeo, get the blood moving."

They knew this was a bunch of crap. I was taken aback that my name was remembered and given a familiar twist. I was embarrassed not to be able to return a proper salutation.

"I need your help to find the Fitz's house, and it was grand that we put up here in this lovely spot and shared a few tugs of the piss, but can we think about moving on soon?"

"Sure, we just have to go see my Ma and Pa and let them know we have a guest from America and we are going to take him a bit down the road to fetch his belongings."

"Do you know where I'm trying to get to?"

"Yea, only a bit away."

I was grateful the boys didn't insist my meeting their folks. Another round of introductions and an inquisition about my stay thus far in Ireland was not appealing. I made some quick work out of removing the soil from my shoe in the wet grass as I waited by the car, and in a whistle the boys were out the back door and we were off.

"Are you sure this is no problem for ya two?"

"Not at all."

I didn't own a timepiece but it was past one hour of daylight. There was a light fog and low cloud cover as we passed along the countryside that showed little or no signs of life at this hour. I checked my pockets and found the same little fold of pounds I received in exchange for twenty dollars at the Shannon Airport three days ago. Hadn't spent a pence.

"Can I give ya a few pounds for gas, the Paddy's, and your help?"

"Save your money for a pint later. You might need it!"

"Are the pubs open on Sunday?"

"Most are, but not until after Mass."

I recognized the buildings ahead on the right as the Fitzgeralds. The car was slowing down before I had a chance to say anything. My heart and head started to throb. What sort of welcome was in store or would I be shunned altogether. I climbed out of the ride and shook hands with the boys. Pleasant goodbyes were exchanged and they made a u-turn and were off.

I was frozen ten feet from the front door. Maybe I should retreat to the field across the way and wait for some time before making any gesture. It was still early after all.

Suddenly, before I could take a single step, the window upstairs above the entrance swung open. There was Mrs. Fitz. She was still in her nightgown and she quickly turned away out of my sight. Then in one swift motion, my bag and its contents were hurled out the window and landed with a thud right at my feet.

She leaned out the window and made the announcement. "Now, James, you know why no Irishman will ever be Pope! Let me fetch my overcoat and I'll be down to give you a ride to the train station."

I was fascinated by this revelation and stood motionless in deep contemplation. Did I play a hand in sealing the fate of all Irish clergy now and forever going forward? In a moment I could hear the car ignite and come swinging out from aside the house. We were on the road driving in silence. The sun had now pierced the layers of cloud and fog and, from knowing my latitude in late October, we were heading south. I admired this woman. I wanted to apologize for being a disruption to their wedding weekend and thank her for all her generosity. Neither of us spoke a word. The road was now approaching a ninety-degree turn to the left, as it did not continue nor was there a crossroad. At the outer edge of this elbow was a modest brick

building alongside a rail line. She pulled into a small gravel turnaround and idled the car in neutral. I waited in silence for at least a minute, then I extended my hand to thank her. She accepted. I was now outside the car, bag by my side.

"Goodbye, Mrs. Fitz and thank you."

She was gone and I turned toward the station. The only activity was an unusually large pigeon population lit on the roof and dozens more circulating. There were two entrances but only one was open. Inside there were some seating areas and a small ticket window that was unattended. There were also no schedules posted. I sat on one of the benches to finally inspect my belongings and look for my money. Nothing had been rearranged and my dough was intact.

The outside bench had a very high back that was exposed to the sun. That seemed inviting and gave me a good view of the rail in both directions and of the road as it continued to the east. It was there that I sat for some time. It was quiet except for the grunting and flapping of the pigeons – too quiet for a train station. Only two cars had passed though the curve on the road bending behind me on the other side of the station since my arrival some half hour ago. I decided to walk out to the road to survey what I would have expected to be an area of activity and saw a figure coming down the road from the east toward the station. A good omen. A fellow passenger was making his way to the station in the middle of nowhere with no schedules or route maps to join me on a train ride to destinations unknown. As he neared I could see he was a proper "Paddy," adorned in the standard irrigation boots, tweed cap and jacket. His gait was long and purposeful and, in a short time, we were directly across the road from each other. I waved and he nodded back, but was not rail-bound, as he was making the turn toward the north. Not a good sign.

"Sir, sir" I hailed. "Can I ask for your help, please?"

He stopped and turned. I briskly crossed to his side of the road and inquired, "Do you know when the train is coming?" His eyes were a blue pair of gems, his jaw pronounced, no sunken mandibles this side of the Irish Sea.

"There are no trains that run from this station on Sunday," he pronounced. "Where are you heading to, lad?"

"Dublin, I hope."

He pointed to the north from where I had come with Mrs. Fitz. "That way to Limerick, then find your way up to Dublin." And with a tip of his cap, he was off.

I sauntered back across the road to grab my bag. It was now endowed with some fresh pigeon shit. A day for adorning excrement. Forge on. I crossed the road back to the bend and started a slow walk toward the north. Within a minute, a car was approaching from the east from whence my Paddy had come. It was moving at a much slower pace than my rescuers' car's pace from outside the pub an eternity ago. I struck the hitchhiker pose and smiled. A nice cream colored four-door sedan rolled to a stop and, after a short exchange, I was in the car agreeing that we were all off to Limerick City this fine Sunday morning.

The gentleman had recently retired from his professorship in history from a prestigious university in Connecticut, and they were on an extended holiday. His wife was a retired homemaker. This was their second time to Ireland, and they had, as millions of Americans do, ancestral ties. Initially, I think they were disappointed that I was a fellow countryman, but when they persisted in wanting to hear about my first impressions – and I told them parts of my first three days on the island, they were interested in every detail, which I was reluctant to share. I don't recall their names, but in telling this story, I always refer to them by the way they were attired – as the "Talbots."

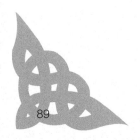

Limerick City was going to be a three-day stop on the Talbots' itinerary. They were planning to see the Cathedral of the Blessed Mary and the university and museums, among other points of interest. Was Mr. Talbot going to be asked to sing at a reception this week? Would he get pissed in a barn and pass out leaving Mrs. Talbot in the lurch at a public house?

I was hoping for a lavatory with running water, perhaps some nourishment other than from a bottle, and a guide to help me move on. Upon our arrival I was struck by the beauty and ruggedness of this town. We had bypassed it the previous Thursday on our way from the airport to the Fitzgeralds. The Talbots were intent on making the last of the Sunday High Mass, and I thought it a good stop, as well, though for different objectives. We made our farewells in the parking lot of the cathedral. I did not want to press on with them, as my agenda was vastly dissimilar.

I saw a street sign that said St. Patrick's Way and another that indicated the way to City Centre. I crossed a bridge over the Shannon River into an area that was abuzz with activity and spotted a sign to a public terminal of sorts. This would have been attractive, but somewhere an intelligence was kicking in. My beloved Steve had taught me certain things, and I had learned a bit on my own. Public transport hubs were not a place to rely on for anything, let alone a reliable restroom. Or transport.

He had taught me something a year earlier on a trip we took together to Chicago. We were walking in the Gold Coast District and he wanted to show me the Tavern at The Drake Hotel. What we both really needed was to pee. He said, "When you need to clean up wherever you are, walk into the finest hotel like you own the joint and make your way to their restroom. No eye contact or directions required." This has served me well.

I don't recall the place, but I washed up, changed my duds and found the hotel bar and restaurant. Soon fortified by a cheese plate, sausage pie and a pint of Guinness, I was road-ready. It wasn't a long walk to find the Christmas tree-style signage that indicated the pathway to Dublin. I was a bit shagged – knackered actually, but determined. I reached near the edge of town before I decided to strike my hitchhiking posture. Again, it was no time before my ride pulled up. An Irishman, middle-aged, quiet and heading home (which was more than halfway to Dublin) was my companion. He wasn't interested in small talk or much about my journey. This was a pleasantry.

The roadway was modest, I thought, for a route connecting two of Ireland's largest towns. Nice two-lane highway that differed from the rural roads I had been transgressing of late. It had an open view and a small shoulder in both directions. Life is a dream. And the dream was slowing down. We passed through small burgs where no stop was required, and late afternoon and the hint of dusk was upon the land. As we slowed at the outskirts of the next burg, there were people dressed in white gowns, carrying torches of some kind, walking the road's shoulder. The modest homes along the town's edge had candle-illuminated shapes on their fences and entrances. It was beautiful. But I had no interest in asking my man what was going on.

Once in the town centre, I asked to be left there. I saw a church and walked to its short staircase to view the arrival of the ghosts from all directions. As night fell, the gathering lit a bonfire that brought a darkness to the entire surroundings. Flames are a dream. When they quieted in the street, I entered the church and made my sleep in the front pew, as a single votive flickered on the side altar.

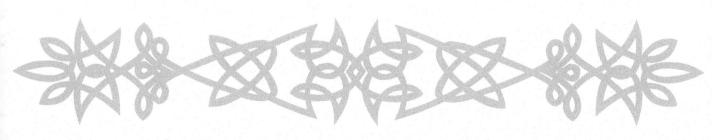

When my grandmother ran the kitchen in my early years, we often ate potatoes. I used to stand next to her at the sink, watching her peel and quarter them. That is when I would eat slices of them raw. Great texture but bland in taste. Cooking all species of potatoes, turnips and squashes, I think, is a good idea. Here are a few favorites that serve 4. These are all loosely written with the notion that many of you will make adaptations to your preference.

Roasted Red Potatoes

Small red potatoes should be round and 2" in diameter and weigh about 3 ounces. These are easy guidelines but not strict.

12 – 14 small red potatoes, each cut into 8 to 10 pieces, leaving the skin on.

Place these into a bowl large enough for them to take a swim in enough olive oil to completely coat.

Season the potatoes with garlic powder, salt-free lemon pepper and black sea salt, mix well.

Spread the potato pieces evenly onto a large cooking sheet and cover generously with sprigs of fresh rosemary and thyme.

Roast for 30 minutes at 375 degrees or longer if necessary until the potatoes are a golden brown and serve.

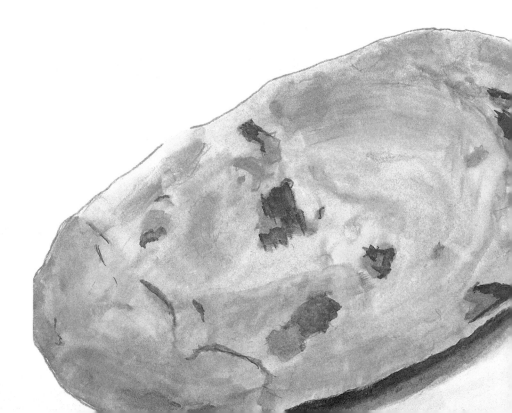

Sweet Potato Crisps

We were eating some sweet potato fries in a restaurant and it was suggested to pour some grated Parmesan and red pepper flakes on them to add some zing. The red peppers are left out of this recipe, but Parmesan is a great twist.

Peel three 12-ounce sweet potatoes and slice into ⅛" rounds and place in a bowl with 4 Tbsp olive oil and 2 Tbsp Italian blend spices. Mix well and season to taste with garlic salt and coarse black pepper

Spread the potato rounds out on flat baking sheet(s) that have been covered with aluminum foil. Place the rounds on the foil so they don't overlap.

Roast for 30 minutes in the oven preheated to 375 degrees. Remove from the oven and check for doneness. They should be cooked but not crisp. Turn up the heat to 425 degrees, lightly coat the rounds with grated Parmesan or your favorite pungent Italian cheeses. Return to the oven for 10 minutes but monitor. These will roast to a crisp quickly. Remove and serve as you like them done. We like ours almost toasted.

Mashed Potatoes

In our kitchen, mashed potatoes are not just the holiday guest from far away seen once a year in November or December. We eat them often and find this recipe our favorite. Use russets. We buy them in the 10-ounce range and about 3" X 5" illustrated herein to spec. For serving 4 people, use 3 spuds as outlined here, and expand to 10 spuds (or about 5 lbs.) for a big crowd, and adjust the other ingredients accordingly.

Peel and quarter 3 potatoes and boil in enough water until tender but not overcooked, about 30 minutes.

Drain all the water and return the pan with the spuds to the stove at low heat.

Add 4 ounces each of softened cream cheese and Half and Half, and 2 ounces of butter.

Season with garlic salt and lemon pepper to taste.

Mash with a potato masher or mixer, your preference. Cover to keep warm until ready to serve.

An additional ingredient that is recommended is fresh shaved Parmesan.

Arborio Rice and Butternut Squash

Peel one medium to large butternut squash, slice in half and remove the seeds and stem. Cut each half lengthwise, and cut each quarter in half again, then slice crosswise to yield roughly 1" X 1" squares. Place these in a bowl with 4 Tbsp olive oil, 5 gloves of minced fresh garlic, Herbs de Provence and sea salt to taste, and mix ingredients well. Roast at 375 for 30-40 minutes. Don't let them over cook or burn. Set aside.

Meanwhile, in a large sauce pan heat 2 Tbsp olive oil on medium heat and add 1 ½ cups of Arborio rice. Stir for 2-3 minutes and add 5 cups of low sodium chicken broth. Mix the ingredients thoroughly and let the mixture come to a boil for 1 minute, reduce heat to low and cook covered for 30 minutes or until done to your liking, set aside.

Pan fry ½ cup pine nuts in enough butter until a light golden brown.

Add the cooked squash and pine nuts to the rice mixture and stir well. Season as needed.

Note: This is a great pairing with Halloween Chicken and a hearty wine.

Mexican Rice

This is as flexible a recipe as there is. Please follow your own taste buds, but if you're curious about how to make a rice that is full of flavor to match Mexican dishes, give this one a try. Si, como no?!

1 ½ cup of uncooked basmati rice. This will serve 6-8 people.

8 Tbsp olive oil

1 cup sweetened coconut milk

2 cups low sodium chicken broth

2 Tbsp cinnamon

2 Tbsp dark chili powder

1 medium yellow onion coarsely chopped

6-8 garlic cloves, peeled and coarsely chopped

2 jalapeno peppers, seeds and stems removed

1 large green bell pepper, seeds and stem removed

4 large tomatoes, best you can find, seeds removed and chopped

1-2 Tbsp ground cumin

brown or raw sugar

1 15-ounce can of cooked red beans

Salt and black pepper

1 In a large saucepan over medium high temperature, heat 4 Tbsp of the olive oil for 1-2 minutes and add the rice, stirring throughout.

2 Add to the rice the coconut milk, broth, cinnamon and chili powder, stirring well. Bring to a boil and reduce heat to low and cover. Cook the rice until done, 30 to 40 minutes.

3 Meanwhile, in a food processor fitted with a steel blade, finely chop the onion, garlic, jalapeños, green pepper, tomatoes and cumin. Don't puree, just a few pulses will do it.

4 Fry the onion mixture in a skillet with the remaining olive oil until the mixture is starting to brown – about 15 minutes on medium low heat.

5 Transfer the fried vegetable mixture to the rice and stir in the red beans. Mix all very thoroughly and continue to cook on low heat for 15 minutes. While stirring, adjust to taste using the cinnamon, raw sugar, etc.

WHAT DO YOU DO AFTER DINNER?

Desserts are not routine for us. They are reserved for special occasions and I'm an infrequent contributor. We do enjoy a finish to great meals, but prefer cheeses, chocolates, nuts and special beverages. Before giving some of those favorites, I will make some suggestions for desserts that we have endorsed, but they're copies of what we found enjoyable from other's efforts.

These are easy and reliable. Try them all.

~Key Lime Pie from Nellie & Joe's Key Lime Juice. Holly gave this one to us and it is flawless.

~Flourless Chocolate Cake straight out of Gourmet Magazine.

~Lemon Snowballs, again Gourmet's version.

DESSERT CHEESES

Cheese is very filling when served as an appetizer and I have been guilty of eating too much of it, leaving me almost disinterested in the main fare. But an array served after dinner paired up with almonds, honey, dates and chocolates and fine sherry or port is a great way to prolong a nice session with friends.

Stiltons, aged Gouda, chevre and Roqueforts top our lists. Differing textures and deep flavors are pleasant when good port is at hand. Some rave about stout red wine. But how do you like a glass of fresh orange juice right after brushing your teeth? Not my choice.

Ports are more accessible than are sherries. And here are two that are spot on. Fonseca's BIN 27 is affordable, delicious and accessible almost anywhere. A second choice is Dow's Old Tawny. If you go for the aged variety, you pay more and may enjoy the rewards.

Sherry wine has so many varieties and price points. It is also mysteriously absent from most of yours and my retailers. Ancient and forgotten. Popular to the area around the city of Cadiz, Spain. Dating nearly 3,000 years back, it traveled the world and went through many transformations. I've drunk my share of some great ones that were reserves at restaurants only to find them absent from my city's best purveyors. The dry varieties such as Lustau Manzanilla are bone dry and pair well with most shellfish, but for dessert go with the deep, dark aromatic varieties.

However, here are a few that I think you can get your hands on with a little effort. The aforementioned Lustau's Pedro Ximenez San Emilio is the ticket. If not locatable, good old Harveys Bristol Cream will do just fine.

CHOCOLATES, PAIRED

If it smells like a bag of cheap Halloween candy, give it to the neighbors' grandchildren. Chocolate is as complex as anything I can think of in the food world and worth stepping it up.

The civilizations of ancient Mexico were so far advanced in calendrics and pharmacology that it astounded Cortes and his soldiers and staff. No wheel or written language, but these people could predict lunar eclipses years in advance to the very hour. Many modern medicines are derivatives of the plants used for similar maladies today by those skilled in their time.

These people cultivated many foodstuffs that were exported back to Europe and were new to the kitchens and tables of Spain. Tomatoes, countless varieties of peppers, vanilla beans, and the most precious of all, the cacao beans. A solid, bitter beverage to Montezuma and his predecessors for many centuries, it was prized for its many attributes and was soon the prize of the Spanish aristocracy who sweetened the drink with honey and vanilla. It took more than three centuries for the Swiss and Dutch to process the beans into what became a piece of chocolate.

Find good chocolate and its many uses. I recommend checking out Cultura Chocolate and their products and approach. Start looking for similar enterprises in your neck of the woods. We like all, but prefer very dark. Almonds, good peanuts, strawberries, chevre and Stilton cheeses are some obvious partners. The higher the cacao content (75% or higher), the better for you if they don't use alkali processing. These flavanols are seriously good stuff for the mind, body and soul.

THAT DAWG LIKES HS CHOCOLATE YEA!